YA 355.825119 SON
Sonneborn, Liz.
The Manhattan Project / Liz
Sonneborn.

D1309537

The Manhattan
Project

MILESTONES
IN MODERN
WORLD HISTORY

The Bolshevik Revolution

The British Industrial Revolution

The Chinese Cultural Revolution

The Collapse of the Soviet Union

D-Day and the Liberation of France

The End of Apartheid in South Africa

The Iranian Revolution

The Manhattan Project

The Mexican Revolution

The Treaty of Nanking

The Treaty of Versailles

The Universal Declaration
of Human Rights

MILESTONES
IN MODERN
WORLD HISTORY

1600 · · · 1750 · · ·

· · · 1940 · · · 2000

The Manhattan Project

FOUNTAINDALE PUBLIC LIBRARY DISTRICT
300 West Briarcliff Road
Bolingbrook, IL 60440-2894
(630) 759-2102

LIZ SONNEBORN

CHELSEA HOUSE
An Infobase Learning Company

The Manhattan Project

Copyright © 2011 by Infobase Learning

All rights reserved. No part of this book may be reproduced or utilized in any form or by any means, electronic or mechanical, including photocopying, recording, or by any information storage or retrieval systems, without permission in writing from the publisher. For information, contact:

Chelsea House
An imprint of Infobase Learning
132 West 31st Street
New York, NY 10001

Library of Congress Cataloging-in-Publication Data

Sonneborn, Liz.
The Manhattan Project / by Liz Sonneborn.
    p.   cm.—(Milestones in world history)
Includes bibliographical references and index.
ISBN 978-1-60413-410-0 (hardcover)
1. Atomic bomb—United States—History—Juvenile literature. 2. Manhattan Project (U.S.)—History—Juvenile literature. I. Title. II. Series.

QC773.3.U5S675 2011
355.8'25119097309044—dc22   2010028916

Chelsea House books are available at special discounts when purchased in bulk quantities for businesses, associations, institutions, or sales promotions. Please call our Special Sales Department in New York at (212) 967-8800 or (800) 322-8755.

You can find Chelsea House on the World Wide Web at http://www.chelseahouse.com.

Text design by Erik Lindstrom
Cover design by Alicia Post
Composition by Keith Trego
Cover printed by Bang Printing, Brainerd, Minn.
Book printed and bound by Bang Printing, Brainerd, Minn.
Date printed: March 2011
Printed in the United States of America

10 9 8 7 6 5 4 3 2 1

This book is printed on acid-free paper.

All links and Web addresses were checked and verified to be correct at the time of publication. Because of the dynamic nature of the Web, some addresses and links may have changed since publication and may no longer be valid.

CONTENTS

Trinity

It was like crossing the Grand Canyon on a tightrope, if the trip took three full years. That is how General Leslie R. Groves described the Manhattan Project in July 1945. Groves headed up this massive government program, which had begun in 1942. The Manhattan Project had one goal—to create an enormously destructive bomb by harnessing the energy within the tiny atom.

When the Manhattan Project was launched, the United States was a relative newcomer to World War II (1939–1945). As the war dragged on, the pressure to develop an atomic bomb grew more urgent. The U.S. government poured huge amounts of money into the Manhattan Project, which maintained facilities across the country. The most crucial was a laboratory at Los Alamos, New Mexico, where many of the world's leading scientists had been struggling night and day to uncover the secrets of atomic energy.

Throughout the project, the Los Alamos scientists had encountered countless obstacles and setbacks. By early 1945, however, all their frustration and hard work finally seemed to be paying off. They had succeeded in designing two types of atomic bombs, although the scientists were not entirely sure their inventions would work. At the urging of the government, they became determined to find out. They made preparations for Trinity—the first test explosion of an atomic weapon. It would be the most elaborate scientific experiment the world had even seen.

PLANNING THE TEST

Preliminary planning for the Trinity test had begun a year before. In March 1944, Kenneth T. Bainbridge, the engineer in charge of the project, had led an expedition into a remote area to the south of Los Alamos. He and his crew tromped over unmapped trails still covered with winter snow. Bainbridge was searching for just the right site for the test.

The area had to be very flat. It also needed to be isolated, miles from any homes or ranches. The scientists at Los Alamos wanted to make sure that the explosion hurt no one and the test was done in secret. Since the inception of the Manhattan Project, the government had done everything possible to shroud it in secrecy out of fear that America's enemies might find out about the weapons research at Los Alamos. The U.S. military now faced its greatest security challenge—hiding the most violent man-made explosion ever from the public. That would be possible only in a place that was virtually unpopulated.

Bainbridge staked out an 18-by-24-mile (29-by-39-kilometer) area in south-central New Mexico. Encompassing the army's Alamogordo Bombing Range, the site was located in a desert basin called the Jornada del Muerto, Spanish for the "Journey of Death." It was given its haunting name by

Workers involved in the top-secret Manhattan Project pose atop a platform stacked with 100 tons (91 metric tons) of TNT prior to the detonation of the first test of an atomic bomb in the New Mexico desert.

seventeenth-century Spaniards, who knew firsthand the hazards of traveling through the dry and barren region.

Workers soon began construction on several buildings at the Trinity site. About five miles (eight km) south of ground zero—the place where the bomb would be detonated—they built barracks and set up tents for military personnel. The area was called Base Camp. They also built three bunkers—one to the north, one to the south, and one to the west—each about six miles (10 km) from ground zero. The north bunker would house instruments to record the blast. The west bunker would store searchlights and cameras to photograph the test. The south bunker would be the headquarters of the scientists and military men directly involved in overseeing the explosion. Bainbridge also designated Compañia Hill, about 20 miles (32 km) away, as a test-viewing site. Important scientists and other dignitaries would be invited to come to Compañia to watch the Trinity test.

At ground zero, Bainbridge supervised the construction of a 20-foot (six-meter) steel tower. On May 7, 1945, his crew carried 100 tons (91 t) of explosives to the top and ignited them. The massive blast allowed Bainbridge to make sure that all his measuring equipment was working properly. Then, at the same site, workers built another, higher tower. This one rose 100 feet (30 m) into the air and was topped by a large platform. When the Trinity test was conducted, the bomb would rest on the firing tower before its detonation.

DOUBTS ABOUT THE BOMB

As the scientists at Los Alamos watched the tower go up, they became more and more nervous. Many had already spent years working on the Manhattan Project. Laboring long hours, day after day, they had puzzled through hundreds of questions that arose in their effort to unleash the power of the atom. All the while, they were under enormous pressure. They knew their answers had to be right. If not, America's enemies could beat them to the bomb and use it to extend their dominance worldwide.

The Los Alamos scientists all shared the same fear—that the Trinity test would prove their invention was a worthless dud. If the bomb failed to explode, they would be devastated. All their hard work would be for nothing. Nearly as bad, however, they would bear the blame for the failure of a project that ultimately cost the U.S. government about $2 billion. Every scientist working on the Manhattan Project secretly feared that, if the bomb were a bust, his work would be blamed for what went wrong.

Some of the senior scientists turned their anxiety into a game. They set up a betting pool. Each man put in a dollar wager and gave his best guess about how much energy the bomb would release, measured in tons of TNT. The man with the closest guess would win the pot. A few made wildly optimistic bets. The famous physicist Edward Teller put his dollar on 45,000 tons (41,000 t), a little less than 10 times what most scientists at Los Alamos thought was a reasonable estimate. Some, though, showed their doubts about their invention with extremely low guesses. Among them was J. Robert Oppenheimer, who was in charge of managing all the scientific work associated with the Manhattan Project. He bet their invention would yield a comparatively measly amount of energy, about 300 tons (272 t) worth.

FEAR OF FAILURE

Oppenheimer was a cautious and thoughtful man. His pessimism might have been the product of exhaustion and frustration. It also, however, might have been based on realities only Oppenheimer could see. No one had worked harder to bring the Manhattan Project to this point, and no one else knew how many things could go wrong. The toll the work had taken on Oppenheimer was clear just by looking at him. Stress, illness, and many late nights had left him emaciated, with only 116 pounds (53 kilograms) on his tall frame.

The Los Alamos scientists had other fears about their bomb. They discussed one possible catastrophic outcome from the Trinity test: the blast would rise up and ignite the atmosphere, destroying the Earth in the process. A thorough examination of the matter ultimately gave them confidence that there was little likelihood this would happen. The idea was so chilling, however, that many scientists could not erase it from their minds.

A more realistic fear focused on the radiation the bomb could release. The Los Alamos scientists believed it would be sent high into the air and therefore not prove a health risk to observers. Still, the radiation threat worried Groves. In case of massive radioactive fallout, he created an evacuation plan to get New Mexico residents to safety. He also talked with the state's governor and recommended that he declare martial law if the evacuation became necessary.

THE TEST DATE NEARS

Groves originally set the test date for July 4, 1945, but because of weather conditions, it was delayed to the early morning hours of July 16. As the day neared, the community of Los Alamos was tense. Elsie McMillan, wife of chemist Edwin M. McMillan, later recalled the anxiety that everyone was feeling: "That last week in many ways dragged, in many ways it flew on wings. It was hard to behave normally. It was hard not to think. It was hard not to let off steam."[1]

According to Oppenheimer, the soldiers stationed at Los Alamos panicked when they saw a strangely bright object in the sky one morning. Fearing it was an enemy plane, they impulsively began shooting at it to take it down. The director of personnel, who was an astronomer, asked Oppenheimer to tell the soldiers to stop firing. The "plane" they were trying to shoot down was the planet Venus.

With the test date nearing, meteorologist Jack M. Hubbard became concerned. He predicted stormy weather on July 16 and suggested that Groves postpone the test again. Groves said no. Harry S. Truman, the president of the United States, wanted to know the results of the test as soon as possible. He was meeting with the leaders of two U.S. allies, Great Britain and the Union of Soviet Socialist Republics (USSR), in Potsdam, Germany. As they began planning their latest war strategy, the president was desperate to know whether the great weapon actually worked.

GETTING THE BOMB TO GROUND ZERO

On July 12, Bainbridge's team began the final stage of preparations for the Trinity test. The bomb, nicknamed the Gadget, was made of a core of plutonium, a man-made element, surrounded by explosives that would crush the core when the bomb went off. At Los Alamos, soldiers gingerly carried the plutonium core to the backseat of an army sedan. They then drove their payload more than 200 miles (322 km) to the Trinity site tower. During the trip, the soldiers treated their precious "passenger" with great care. The plutonium had taken scientists years to produce at a cost of millions of dollars to the government.

The next step was to transport the rest of the bomb assembly. The following day, however, was Friday the thirteenth. Not wanting to jinx the test, George Kistiakowsky, head of the project's implosion department, decided to begin the drive one minute after midnight, bypassing the traditionally unlucky day. During the late-night drive, Kistiakowsky briefly snoozed. He woke with a jolt to the sound of the car's screaming siren. As they were passing through the city of Santa Fe, the driver decided it was prudent to turn on the siren to alert any drunken drivers of their presence. If the car were involved in an accident, the workings of the bomb could have set off an enormous explosion in the city's center.

TESTING THE TEST

On Saturday, several scientists, at Oppenheimer's request, fired a copy of the bomb, designed to test whether the Trinity bomb would go off as planned. To their horror, their test showed that the Trinity bomb would fail. According to their calculations, the Gadget would not explode properly, and the Trinity test would be an embarrassing disaster.

The news was hardly what Oppenheimer wanted to hear. He was in the city of Albuquerque, where a group of army generals and famed scientists were being wined and dined in anticipation of the Trinity demonstration. That night, Oppenheimer returned to Base Camp, but he was so overwhelmed with worry that he could barely sleep.

The physicist Hans Bethe was also awake. Obsessed by the results of the implosion test, he stayed up all night, running through the calculations. By Sunday morning, he had encouraging news. The disappointing results of the test were not the fault of the Trinity bomb, Bethe decided. They arose from flaws with the test itself. Bethe's last-minute brainwork persuaded everyone, even Oppenheimer, that there was a good chance the Gadget would work after all.

LAST-MINUTE PREPARATIONS

The weather, however, was still not cooperating. Hubbard met with Oppenheimer, Groves, and Bainbridge at 4 o'clock on Sunday afternoon. He complained that the weather was too stormy for the planned detonation at 4 A.M. Monday. Although annoyed at the news, Groves agreed to reassess the situation two hours before the scheduled test time.

At 5 P.M. on Sunday, the fully assembled bomb was hoisted to the top of the tower. An exhausted Oppenheimer made his final inspection of ground zero. Satisfied that everything was going according to plan, Oppenheimer headed off to the south bunker, from which he would watch the test.

Oppenheimer, though, still harbored fears that America's enemies might somehow try to sabotage the test. He decided someone had to "babysit" the Gadget through the night. He chose a young scientist named Don Hornig for the task. As Hornig later recalled, "I don't know if it was that I was most expendable or best able to climb a 100-foot tower!"[2] In any case, he spent the night on the tower platform, in the tiny shelter there, sitting next to a plutonium bomb. Hornig later joked about his inadequate preparation to protect it from anyone. He was armed with nothing but a book and a folding chair.

Not surprisingly, Hornig had an exceptionally tense evening. Many of the other scientists at Los Alamos also felt on edge. Isidor I. Rabi distracted himself by playing poker. Emilio Segré read a French novel before settling into bed. With a heavy dose of black humor, Enrico Fermi joked around with his fellow scientists at Base Camp. He offered to take bets on what would be destroyed if the bomb set the atmosphere ablaze—just New Mexico or the entire world. Bainbridge was annoyed. He worried that the military personnel who were not as familiar with the science of the bomb would not understand that Fermi was joking.

By about 2 in the morning, the thunderstorms Hubbard had predicted began. Hornig was uneasy. At the top of a 100-foot (30-m) steel tower in a desert basin, he worried about lightning strikes. He tried to comfort himself with the idea that if lightning hit and detonated bomb, he would be dead long before he knew what had happened.

WEATHERING THE STORMS

When the storms started, Hubbard was taking his final measurements at the tower. He then went to the south bunker to confer with Groves and Oppenheimer. Groves was angry. He lashed out at Hubbard, shouting "What the hell is wrong with the weather?"[3] Oppenheimer stepped in. After years of managing complex people dealing with complex problems, he instinctively tried to calm everyone's raw nerves. Hubbard wanted to delay the detonation to between 5 and 6 A.M. Oppenheimer urged Groves to take his advice, reminding Groves that Hubbard was enormously skilled at his job. Trusting Oppenheimer, Groves agreed, but not before telling Hubbard, "You'd better be right on this, or I will hang you."[4]

Groves rescheduled the test for 5:30 A.M. He later recalled how he and Oppenheimer spent the early morning hours.

Together, they repeatedly checked the weather, walking "out into the darkness to look at the stars and to assure each other that the one or two visible stars were becoming brighter."[5] According to Groves's deputy, Brigadier General Thomas F. Farrell, Groves did his best to comfort Oppenheimer whenever he became agitated: "Every time the Director [Oppenheimer] would be about to explode because of some untoward happening, General Groves would take him off and walk with him in the rain, counseling with him and reassuring him that everything would be all right."[6]

A NERVOUS WAIT

At about 5:10 A.M., Groves left the south bunker and headed for Base Camp. The camp was closer to ground zero and therefore provided a better observation point. Groves also wanted to be in a different location than Oppenheimer when the bomb exploded. They knew more about the Manhattan Project than anyone else. If somehow everyone at Base Camp were wiped out by the blast, he had to be sure Oppenheimer would survive to carry on their work.

In the meantime, the distinguished guests stationed at Compañia Hill nervously waited to view the explosion. The countdown of minutes was broadcast over a loudspeaker, but those on the hill were too far away to hear it. They instead relied on a radio broadcast, but their radio was not working properly. The young physicist Richard Feynman had loved fiddling with radios as a child. Remembering his childhood hobby, he tinkered with the broken equipment until the countdown came through loud and clear.

As the minutes ticked away, the atmosphere on the hill grew tenser still. According to Ernest O. Lawrence, "With the darkness and the waiting in the chill of the desert the tension became almost unendurable."[7] Many started fiddling with the dark sunglasses and pieces of welders' glass they had brought to shield their eyes from the intense burst of light the bomb would release. As a precaution, Teller passed around a bottle of suntan lotion, which guests rubbed on their faces and hands while standing in the dark. The guests had been instructed to lie down on the ground with their faces turned away from the blast. According to Teller, however, "No one complied. We were determined to look the beast in the eye."[8] The men at Base Camp were not so cavalier about the instructions they were given. In the final moments of the countdown, they all lay down in trenches with their feet facing ground zero.

"A FLOOD OF SUNLIGHT"

Finally the waiting was over. At precisely 5:30 A.M., the countdown ended. A tremendous burst of light filled the morning sky, a light brighter than any before seen by human beings. Teller said it "was like opening the heavy curtains of a darkened room to a flood of sunlight."[9] Even at faraway Compañia Hill, the light was so intense that it temporarily blinded one scientist who dared to stare at it with unprotected eyes. At Base Camp, the "unbelievable brightness" so startled Segré that he feared it marked the end of the world: "I believe that for a moment I thought the explosion might set fire to the atmosphere and thus finish the earth, even though I knew that this was not possible."[10]

After that initial blast of light, the observers watched a huge ball of debris rise and spread in the air. Another smaller ball rose up beneath it. Because of the shape they formed, the image became known as a mushroom cloud. To many who saw it, the first mushroom cloud was beautiful. "It was golden, purple, violet, gray and blue," Farrell later wrote. "It lighted every peak, crevasse and ridge of the nearby mountain range with a clarity and beauty that cannot be described."[11] Others, however, such as Rabi, were chilled by what they saw: "[T]here was an enormous ball of fire which grew and grew and it rolled as it grew; it went up into the air, in yellow flashes and into scarlet and green. It looked menacing."[12]

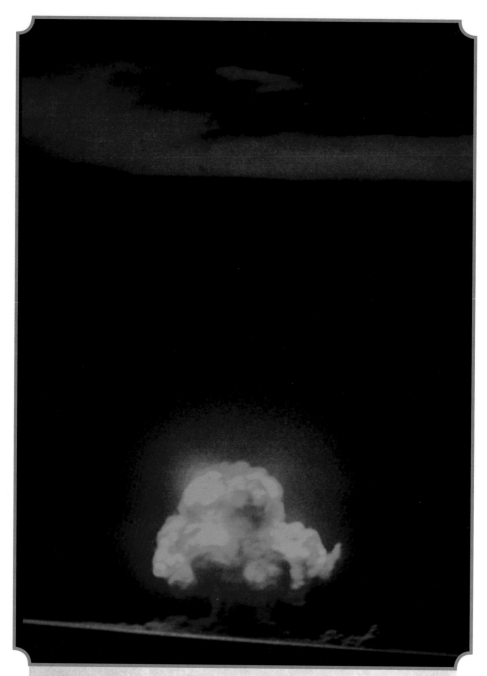

The successful test of the world's first atomic bomb, code named Trinity, at a location about 35 miles (56 kilometers) southeast of Socorro, New Mexico, on July 16, 1945, far exceeded many of its designers' expectations.

About 30 seconds after the explosion, a huge blast of air rushed over the New Mexican desert. It was followed by a great booming roar that echoed back as the sound waves ricocheted off the nearby mountains. When the air blast reached Compañia Hill, Fermi sprinkled some slips of paper into the powerful wind. They landed several meters away. After measuring the distance, he pulled out a table of numbers he had prepared earlier. From the table, he determined that the energy released from the bomb equaled an explosion of 10,000 tons (9,000 t) of TNT. His simple experiment suggested that the plutonium bomb was an extremely powerful weapon.

REFLECTIONS ON THE BOMB

Even without Fermi's calculations, Oppenheimer knew the Trinity test was an astounding success. Farrell recalled how, as soon as Oppenheimer heard the explosion's boom, "his face relaxed into an expression of tremendous relief."[13] In the south bunker, Kistiakowsky threw his arms around Oppenheimer and all the other scientists let out a loud cheer.

Oppenheimer then headed toward Base Camp, where he found a similar celebration going on. Rabi passed around a bottle of whiskey while the scientists and military men all congratulated one another. Groves greeted Oppenheimer with the words, "I am proud of you."[14] Oppenheimer was just as pleased with himself. Farrell later wrote that as Oppenheimer approached the camp, "his walk was like . . . this kind of strut. He'd done it."[15]

Soon, though, the mood at Base Camp darkened. The cheers and congratulations became muted as the relieved men gave themselves over to their exhaustion. It was not just the fatigue of the tense day that quieted their celebration. It was the sobering sense of what they had done, what their success in building the first atomic bomb could mean to the world. Their unease only grew as they analyzed their measurements of the blast's

(continues on page 23)

"UNPRECEDENTED, MAGNIFICENT, BEAUTIFUL, STUPENDOUS, AND TERRIFYING"

Brigadier General Thomas F. Farrell served as a deputy to General Leslie R. Groves, head of the Manhattan Project. Groves asked Farrell to record his impressions of the Trinity test, which Groves then forwarded with his own account to Secretary of War Henry L. Stimson. The following is an excerpt from his report:

The scene inside the shelter was dramatic beyond words. In and around the shelter were some twenty-odd people concerned with last minute arrangements prior to firing the shot. . . .

[A]nnouncements began to be broadcast of the interval remaining before the blast. They were sent by radio to the other groups participating in and observing the test. As the time interval grew smaller and changed from minutes to seconds, the tensions increased by leaps and bounds. Everyone in that room knew the awful potentialities of the thing that they thought was about to happen. . . . We were reaching into the unknown and we did not know what might come of it. . . .

[W]hen the announcer shouted "Now!" and there came a tremendous burst of light followed shortly thereafter by the deep growling roar of the explosion, [J. Robert Oppenheimer's] face relaxed into an expression of tremendous relief. Several of the observers standing [in the] back of the shelter to watch the lighting effects were knocked flat by the blast.

The tension in the room let up and all started congratulating each other. Everyone sensed "This is it!" No matter what might happen now all knew that the impossible scientific job had been done. . . .

All the pent-up emotions were released in those few minutes and all seemed to sense immediately that the explosion had far exceeded the most optimistic expectations and wildest hopes of the scientists. All seemed to feel that they had been present at the birth of a new age—The Age of Atomic Energy—and felt their profound responsibility to help in guiding into right channels the tremendous forces which had been unlocked for the first time in history. . . .

The effects could well be called unprecedented, magnificent, beautiful, stupendous, and terrifying. No man-made phenomenon of such tremendous power had ever occurred before. The lighting effects beggared description. The whole country was lighted by a searing light with the intensity many times that of the midday sun. It was golden, purple, violet, gray and blue. It lighted every peak, crevasse and ridge of the nearby mountain range with a clarity and beauty that cannot be described but must be seen to be imagined. It was that beauty that great poets dream about but describe most poorly and inadequately. Thirty seconds after the explosion came first, the air blast pressing hard against people and things, to be followed almost immediately by the strong, sustained, awesome roar which warned of doomsday and made us feel that we puny things were blasphemous to dare tamper with the forces heretofore reserved to the Almighty. Words are inadequate tools for the jobs of acquainting those not present with the physical, mental and psychological effects. It had to be witnessed to be realised.*

* Cynthia C. Kelly, ed., *The Manhattan Project: The Birth of the Atomic Bomb in the Words of Its Creators, Eyewitnesses, and Historians.* New York: Black Dog & Leventhal Publishers, 2007, pp. 294-296.

J. Robert Oppenheimer, the American physicist and scientific director of the Manhattan Project, and Major General Leslie Groves, the project's military director, inspect the aftermath of the atomic test site in New Mexico.

(continued from page 19)
strength. Fermi's paper scrap experiment had underestimated the bomb's power. Its energy yield was the equivalent of 21,000 tons (19,000 t) of TNT, more than twice what he had estimated.

The news was especially disturbing to Oppenheimer. He was not just a scientist, but also a philosopher and seeker. He had long been a student of the Bhagavad Gita, an ancient text sacred to Hindus. As he reflected on the awesome power of atomic bomb—the weapon he had been so instrumental in creating—a declaration by the supreme being Vishnu from the Bhagavad Gita began to haunt his thoughts: "Now I am become Death, the destroyer of worlds."[16]

Energy and the Atom

The idea that all matter is composed of discrete units—known as atoms—is an ancient one. The Greek philosopher Leucippus first developed the concept in the fifth century B.C. He theorized that if you split a piece of matter over and over again, you would eventually end up with an atom, a fundamental particle that cannot be divided. The name "atomists" was given to Greek thinkers who believed Leucippus's theory.

By the nineteenth century, generally all physicists—scientists who study the properties of matter and energy—were "atomists." They believed there were 92 naturally occurring chemical substances, known as elements, which included hydrogen, oxygen, carbon, silver, iron, and uranium. Physicists also held that each element was made of atoms of the same structure. They, like Leucippus, thought that it was impossible to divide an atom into anything smaller.

ATOMIC MODELS

In 1897, this concept of the atom was challenged by J.J. Thomson, a physicist working at the Cavendish Laboratory at Cambridge University in England. Using electromagnetic force, Thomson was able to separate negatively charged particles from atoms. His experiments proved that the atom was, in fact, divisible and introduced the world to the first known subatomic particle: the electron.

Atoms themselves hold no electrical charge, which prompted Thomson to propose a new model of the atom. He envisioned atoms as a collection of electrons imbedded in a sphere with a positive charge, which canceled out the electrons' negative charge. Thomson's theory was named after a traditional English dessert called plum pudding—a round moist cake usually flavored with bits of dried fruit. According to Thomson's plum pudding model, the cake represented the positively charged sphere of the atom, while the fruit inside represented the atom's negatively charged electrons.

The plum pudding model was soon disputed by one of Thomson's own students, an exuberant young physicist from New Zealand named Ernest Rutherford. Working at England's University of Manchester, Rutherford discovered that the positive charge of an atom was concentrated in what became known as its nucleus. The nucleus sat in the center of an atom and accounted for almost all of its mass. According to Rutherford, the relatively tiny electrons orbit around the nucleus just as the planets in our solar system orbit around the Sun. As a result, Rutherford's concept of the atom became known as the planetary model.

BOHR'S DISCOVERIES

Rutherford's planetary model, however, seemed flawed. According to the traditional law of physics, the orbiting electrons would eventually lose energy and come crashing into the nucleus. This did not happen. Instead, most atoms were extremely stable.

Niels Bohr made fundamental contributions to mankind's understanding of atomic structure and quantum mechanics, for which he received the Nobel Prize in Physics in 1922. During World War II, Bohr worked on the Manhattan Project.

A Danish physicist named Niels Bohr, who came to Manchester to study with Rutherford, began to investigate this inconsistency. Rutherford was an experimental physicist, well known for the elegant design of his lab experiments. Bohr, however, was a theoretical physicist who explored physical phenomena not through experiments but through abstract thought and mathematical equations. Rutherford generally did not like theoreticians, but he embraced the affable and athletic Bohr. "Bohr's different," he once jokingly proclaimed, "He's a football player!"[1]

Using Rutherford's experimental data and the recent theoretical work of physicists Max Planck and Albert Einstein, Bohr discovered what was wrong with the planetary model of the atom—nothing. Instead, the classical laws of physics were the problem. Bohr found that on the *atomic* level particles behaved according to a different set of rules. Bohr's research created an entirely new branch of physics known as quantum mechanics, which explains the behavior of subatomic particles.

In 1921, Bohr founded the Institute for Theoretical Physics at the University of Copenhagen in Denmark. The following year, he was awarded the Nobel Prize in Physics and made another great discovery: he found that electrons traveled around the nucleus in nested shells and that each shell could hold only so many electrons at a given time. These observations formed the basis of the Bohr model of the atom.

INSIDE THE NUCLEUS

Rutherford continued his laboratory work on atomic structure. In 1919, he had detected a nuclear particle with a positive charge, which became known as the proton. The discovery of the proton not only added to the understanding of the atom but also provided a tool to learn more about the atom's structure. Physicists could now probe the atom by bombarding the nucleus with protons.

Working with his assistant James Chadwick, Rutherford used protons to investigate the properties of atoms of different elements. They had success with atoms of lighter elements, such as hydrogen, which had only one proton. They ran into trouble, however, with heavier elements, such as uranium, whose atoms contained 92 protons. The reason was that the bombarding proton and the protons in the nucleus were both positively charged. Particles with the same electrical charge naturally repel each other. In the hydrogen atom, with a single proton, this repulsion is not strong enough keep the bombarding proton from penetrating the nucleus. In the uranium atom with 92 protons, however, the nucleus creates a strong electronic barrier that deflects the proton.

Physicists began to speculate that if they could find a way to increase the speed of bombarding protons, they could break the barrier and penetrate heavy nuclei (the plural of nucleus). They talked of building large machines to accelerate particles. Rutherford, preferring his carefully designed simple experiments, disdained this avenue of research, but it inspired Ernest O. Lawrence, a young American physicist looking to make a name for himself. Like many American scientists and engineers, Lawrence had grown up tinkering with radios and teaching himself about radio technology. The largely mechanical problem of building an accelerator had a natural appeal for him. Fortunately for Lawrence, the United States, with a thriving industrial base, was the best place to develop "big-machine physics." In 1932, at the Berkeley Radiation Laboratory in California, Lawrence designed the first cyclotron—a particle accelerator that uses electromagnetic force to move a proton around and around in a circle to increase the particle's speed.

FINDING THE NEUTRON

The same year, back in England, Rutherford's assistant James Chadwick made another astounding breakthrough. Rutherford had long speculated that atoms contained more than

Ernest O. Lawrence of the University of California, Berkeley, built the first cyclotron in 1932. Since 1929, he had been working on a way to produce particles sufficiently energetic for nuclear reactions. Lawrence decided to accelerate his particles in a spiral path within a pair of semi-cylinders mounted in a vacuum between the poles of an electromagnet.

just protons and electrons. He thought there might also exist a neutral subatomic particle in the nucleus—one with mass, like the proton, but with no electrical charge. While managing Rutherford's laboratory, Chadwick began looking into this question in his spare time.

A report in a French scientific journal on work conducted by married French physicists Irène and Frédéric Joliot-Curie inspired Chadwick to conduct a series of experiments in search of the neutral particle. Convinced he was on the brink of a major discovery, he worked 10 days straight with very little sleep before finding evidence that the particle did actually exist. On the morning of February 17, 1932, he sent a letter to the editor of *Nature* magazine to announce the discovery of what came to be known as the neutron. That night, the exhausted Chadwick met with a group of physicists and delivered what an eyewitness called "one of the shortest accounts ever made about a major discovery."[2] He concluded his startling but brief statement with, "Now I want to be . . . put to bed for a fortnight [two weeks]."[3]

The discovery of the neutron was momentous. It finally solved the problem of the heavy nuclei repelling bombarding protons. The uncharged neutron could be shot directly into a nucleus with no electronic barrier to overcome. The neutron, therefore, finally gave physicists a tool with which they could break up atoms and see what was inside.

Chadwick's neutron also explained a mystery that had long puzzled physicists: how could atoms of the same element exist in different weights? The answer was that heavier versions had more neutrons. Different types of atoms of the same element became known as isotopes. For instance, uranium was found to have three isotopes—one with 142 neutrons, one with 143, and one with 146.

PHYSICISTS IN HITLER'S GERMANY

With the invention of the cyclotron and the discovery of the neutron, the world of physics was changing fast. At the same time, many European physicists found themselves caught up in a political upheaval. On January 30, 1933, Adolf Hitler became the chancellor of Germany. He made sweeping changes in the government, many of which sought to strip German Jews of their civil rights. Hitler came to power in part because of his anti-Semitism, or hatred of Jewish people. Since Germany's defeat in World War I (1914–1918), the country's economy had been in shambles, leading to widespread misery. Like Hitler, many Germans wrongly blamed their nation's Jewish population for Germany's problems.

Many German physicists who were Jewish scrambled to leave the country, especially after Hitler prohibited Jews from working at universities. Among them was Leo Szilard, a Hungarian-born inventor and physics instructor at the University of Berlin. In 1933, Szilard fled to London, England, with a little cash and no job prospects. While drinking coffee one morning, he scanned the London *Times* and saw an article about a speech Ernest Rutherford had recently given. Rutherford had talked about the discovery of the neutron, what it meant for the future of physics, and how the neutron could be used to create energy.

According to this idea, if an atom's nucleus was bombarded with neutrons, some matter in the nucleus could be transformed into energy. This was based on Einstein's famous formula $E=mc^2$, in which E stands for energy, m stands for mass, and c^2 stands for the speed of light squared (90,000,000,000 kilometers per second). The equation states that matter and energy are equivalent—that is, that matter can become energy and energy can become matter. It also indicates that, because c^2 is such a huge number, even a tiny amount of matter could theoretically create an enormous amount of energy.

Rutherford found the idea interesting in theory, but he deeply doubted that any scientist would be able to create nuclear energy anytime soon. He was not alone in this opinion. Other great physicists, including Einstein and Bohr, also dismissed the idea.

The article about Rutherford's speech annoyed Szilard. As he later recalled, "Lord Rutherford was reported to have said that whoever talks about the liberation of atomic energy on an industrial scale is talking moonshine. Pronouncements of experts to the effect that something cannot be done have always irritated me."[4]

BOMBARDING THE NUCLEUS

With no work and plenty of time on his hands, Szilard began thinking about nuclear energy. Walking around London one

THE EXODUS FROM GERMANY

On April 11, 1933, the government of Germany, headed by Chancellor Adolf Hitler, declared that only "Aryans" (non-Jewish whites) would be allowed to work at state institutions, including universities. The law, which forced the firing of Jewish professors and other professionals, would have a sweeping impact on the international community of physicists.

Because of the law, about a quarter of the physicists in Germany were dismissed from their jobs. They lost not only their source of income but also their access to laboratories where they could perform experiments. Many German physicists felt they had no choice but to leave their native land. As theoretical physicist Edward Teller explained:

> It was a foregone conclusion that I had to leave. After all, not only was I a Jew, I was not even a German citizen. I wanted to be a scientist. The possibility to remain a scientist in Germany and to have any chance of continuing to work had vanished with the coming of Hitler. I had to leave, as many others did, as soon as I could.*

day, he stopped at an intersection and waited for the light to change. When it turned green, he stepped into the street, and an idea popped into his mind: "[I]t . . . suddenly occurred to me that if we could find an element which is split by neutrons and which would emit *two* neutrons when it absorbs *one* neutron, such an element, if assembled in sufficiently large mass, could sustain a nuclear chain reaction."[5] In such a chain reaction, a neutron would strike a nucleus, releasing energy and more neutrons. Those neutrons would then strike other nuclei, releasing still more energy and more neutrons. If the reaction

Physicists in other countries worked hard to get their colleagues out of Germany and find them work elsewhere. Danish physicist Niels Bohr, for instance, traveled to Germany to seek out scientists who needed aid. He also established a summer conference at his institute in Copenhagen, in part to help German physicists escape and seek out new jobs. One exile, Otto Frisch, described the conference as "a confusing affair, with so many people and so little time to sort them out."**

Organizations also emerged to help the fleeing scholars. In the United States, private donors created the Faculty Fellowship Fund at Columbia University, and the Institute for International Education established the Emergency Committee in Aid of Displaced German Scholars. As a result, about 100 European physicists immigrated to the United States between 1933 and 1941. Although it was not clear at the time, this migration of learned scientists would soon have an important impact on world history.

---

* Richard Rhodes, *The Making of the Atomic Bomb*. New York: Simon & Schuster, 1986, pp. 189-190.
** Ibid., p. 193.

continued, it would be possible to create an enormous explosion. Before reaching the curb, Szilard had envisioned a horrible new weapon—an atomic bomb.

At any time, the idea would have been disturbing. With Hitler becoming more powerful by the day, however, for Szilard, the thought was absolutely horrifying. He knew there were many skilled physicists still in Germany. He worried they might be thinking the same thing he was. It seemed all too possible that someday they might figure out how to build an atomic bomb and place it in Hitler's hands.

Szilard was eager to experiment with different elements to test his idea. That, however, required funding and access to a laboratory, neither of which he had. Instead Enrico Fermi, a 33-year-old physicist in Rome, Italy, took up that work. At the time, Italy did not have much of a reputation in physics, and Fermi was determined to change that. Intrigued by the possibilities of the neutron, he and his team of researchers successfully bombarded atoms of 63 elements with the neutron and created new elements not found in nature. All of these elements were radioactive, meaning that their nuclei were unstable. Fermi and his colleagues also discovered how to slow neutrons during the bombardment process, which yielded better results.

Fermi found that the nuclei of most atoms were somewhat altered after being hit by neutrons. Uranium nuclei, however, were completely changed. They appeared to break into two almost equal pieces. What exactly happened to the uranium atoms was not clear to Fermi or to any other nuclear physicists. The question would continue to trouble and intrigue the international physics community over the next few years.

FISSION DISCOVERED

In late 1938, two German chemists—Otto Hahn and Fritz Strassman—were conducting their own nuclear bombardment experiments at the Kaiser Wilhelm Institute in Berlin, Germany. Following Fermi's lead, they experimented with uranium. When they bombarded uranium atoms with neutrons, they found traces of radioactive isotopes of the element barium in their results. Also, the products of their uranium experiments collectively weighed less than the original uranium had. Hahn and Strassman thought they had discovered something, but they were not sure what.

Hahn decided to consult an old friend and colleague, Lise Meitner. A renowned Austrian physicist, Meitner was the second woman ever to be awarded a Ph.D. at the University of Vienna. Until recently, she had been a professor in Berlin, but, as a Jew, she was forced out of her job by Germany's anti-Semitic laws. With Hahn's help, she had escaped to Stockholm, Sweden.

When Hahn wrote Meitner about his experiment, she was on Christmas vacation with her nephew Otto Frisch, a fellow physicist and German exile living in Copenhagen. Meitner was fascinated by Hahn's experiment results. She shared his letter with her nephew and insisted that they spend their vacation trying to figure out what the results meant. During long winter walks through the Swedish countryside, they puzzled over the baffling data.

Their calculations finally revealed that Hahn and Strassman had done something amazing: They had succeeded in splitting the uranium atom in half. The result was not something that just looked like new atoms. It *was* new atoms. Their split uranium atom had produced an atom of a barium isotope and an atom of krypton. The two resulting atoms weighed less than the original uranium atom because, when the uranium atom broke apart, some of the atom's matter had been converted into energy. Frisch named this process nuclear fission. The discovery of fission suggested that Rutherford, Bohr, and Einstein had been wrong. Perhaps physicists would soon be able to figure out how to harness the power of the atom to create energy.

AN UNCERTAIN FUTURE

Meitner and Frisch were stunned. They could hardly believe what their calculations said. Could they be wrong? Just to be sure, they decided to consult with Niels Bohr. Returning to Copenhagen, Frisch showed their work to the great Danish physicist. Frisch later recalled Bohr's response: "I had hardly begun to tell him, when he struck his forehead with his hand and exclaimed, 'Oh what idiots we have all been! Oh but this is wonderful! This is just as it must be!' "[6]

Bohr was about to sail for New York City. He took the calculations with him on his trip. During the voyage, he checked Meitner and Frisch's work and confirmed that their calculations were correct. In January 26, 1939, just 10 days after arriving in the United States, Bohr addressed a gathering of scientists at a conference on theoretical physics in Washington, D.C., and told the crowd about fission. News of the discovery spread throughout scientific communities in America and Europe. Physicists everywhere began working with feverish excitement, all trying to learn more about fission and imagining what the discovery might mean for the world of science.

When Leo Szilard heard about fission, he was visiting a friend at Princeton University in New Jersey. The physicists there were excited by the news. According to Szilard, "The Department of Physics at Princeton . . . was like a stirred-up ant heap."[7] He, however, had trouble sharing their enthusiasm. Szilard could not help remembering that day back in London when, while crossing a busy street, he had suddenly envisioned a tremendous and horrible atomic bomb. The discovery of fission brought that vision in his head one step closer to becoming a reality. Rather than celebrating the news, Szilard predicted that the world was headed for grief.

Sounding the Alarm

The news about fission was not the only thing that disturbed Leo Szilard. He was also upset that Bohr, in his conference address, had openly discussed the idea of a nuclear chain reaction, which, if properly controlled, could create an atomic bomb. Szilard believed that talking publicly about the subject was irresponsible. He did not think American and European physicists should reveal any information that could help German scientists working for Hitler's regime to create such a bomb. Szilard felt that if his colleagues were involved in nuclear research, they had a moral obligation to work in secrecy.

Szilard tried to get other nuclear physicists to agree to a voluntary ban on publishing papers about their work. With a friend, physicist Isidor I. Rabi, Szilard visited Enrico Fermi to get his support. Fermi, whose wife was Jewish, had escaped his native Italy and its anti-Semitic laws. He had settled in New York City, where he worked in the laboratories at Columbia University. Fermi listened carefully to Szilard and Rabi's arguments but remained unconvinced. Instead of censoring their work, Fermi argued, physicists should just play down the importance of a nuclear chain reaction. After all, Fermi told them, there was probably only about a 10 percent chance anyone would ever be able to create one that could power a bomb. Rabi responded, "Ten per cent is not a remote possibility if it means that we may die of it. If I have pneumonia and the doctor tells that there is a remote possibility that I might die, and it's ten percent, I get excited about it."[1]

Unable to persuade Fermi, Szilard set out to convince Niels Bohr in March 1939. He enlisted the help of Edward Teller and Eugene Wigner, two physicist friends who, like Szilard, were Hungarians who had fled from Germany. The three men made their case to Bohr, but he said the point was moot. No one was ever going to have the resources needed to build an atomic bomb. According to Teller, Bohr said that "it can never be done unless you turn the United States into one huge factory."[2]

Bohr also resisted the idea of hiding experiment results. For many years, he had encouraged physicists of all nationalities to work together to solve common problems. As much as he feared Hitler, he felt physics should be kept free of politics.

HELP FROM EINSTEIN

By July 1939, Szilard, Wigner, and Teller decided they had to inform the U.S. government that Germany might be building an atomic bomb. They also wanted to alert the government of Belgium. Belgium then controlled the African country known as the Belgian Congo (now the Democratic Republic of the Congo), which had substantial deposits of uranium. The three physicists felt they needed to warn Belgium against selling uranium to the Germans.

In this circa-1946 photo, Albert Einstein *(left)* and Leo Szilard re-enact the signing of their 1939 letter to President Franklin D. Roosevelt, in which they warned him that Nazi Germany could have been building an atomic bomb.

With both these goals in mind, Szilard, Wigner, and Teller contacted Albert Einstein, then the most respected scientist in the world. He also was a personal friend of the Queen of Belgium. Einstein invited the three men to visit him at his summer home in Long Island, New York, on a hot Sunday afternoon. There they told Einstein about the latest experiments in nuclear fission, of which he was largely unaware. A German exile of Jewish ancestry, Einstein was concerned about Hitler getting a new weapon and agreed to help. With Szilard's

(continues on page 42)

A LETTER TO THE PRESIDENT

Probably the most famous scientist in the world at the time, Albert Einstein, sent a letter to President Franklin D. Roosevelt on August 2, 1939. In it, he alerted the president to a growing threat—that Germany, under the rule of Adolf Hitler, was working to employ nuclear science to create a massively powerful bomb.

Sir:

Some recent work by E. Fermi and L. Szilard, which has been communicated to me in manuscript, leads me to expect that the element uranium may be turned into a new and important source of energy in the immediate future. Certain aspects of the situation which has arisen seem to call for watchfulness and, if necessary, quick action on the part of the Administration. I believe therefore that it is my duty to bring to your attention the following facts and recommendations.

In the course of the last four months it has been made probable—through the work of Joliot in France as well as Fermi and Szilard in America—that it may be possible to set up a nuclear chain reaction in a large mass of uranium by which vast amounts of power and large quantities of new radium-like elements would be generated. Now it appears almost certain that this could be achieved in the immediate future.

This phenomenon would also lead to the construction of bombs, and it is conceivable—though much less certain— that extremely powerful bombs of a new type may thus be constructed. A single bomb of this type, carried by boat and exploded in a port, might very well destroy the whole port together with some of the surrounding territory. . . .

In view of this situation you may think it desirable to have some permanent contact maintained between the

Administration and the group of physicists working on chain reactions in America. One possible way of achieving this might be for you to entrust with the task a person who has your confidence and who could perhaps serve in an unofficial capacity. His task might comprise the following:

a) to approach Government Departments, keep them informed of the further development, and put forward recommendations for Government action, giving particular attention to the problem of securing a supply of uranium ore for the United States.

b) to speed up the experimental work, which is at present being carried on within the limits of the budgets of University laboratories, by providing funds, if such funds be required, through his contacts with private persons who are willing to make contributions for this cause, and perhaps also by obtaining the co-operation of industrial laboratories which have the necessary equipment.

I understand that Germany has actually stopped the sale of uranium from the Czechoslovakian mines which she has taken over. That she should have taken such early action might perhaps be understood on the ground that the son of the German Under-Secretary of State, von Weizsäcker, is attached to the Kaiser-Wilhelm-Institut in Berlin where some of the American work on uranium is now being repeated.

Yours very truly,
    Albert Einstein*

---

* Cynthia C. Kelly, ed., *The Manhattan Project: The Birth of the Atomic Bomb in the Words of Its Creators, Eyewitnesses, and Historians*. New York: Black Dog & Leventhal Publishers, 2007, pp. 43–44.

(continued from page 39)
input, he drafted a letter about the matter to President Franklin D. Roosevelt.

On August 15, Szilard gave the letter to Alexander Sachs, a wealthy financier who was a friend and adviser to Roosevelt. Sachs agreed to hand deliver it to the president, but it took him two months to get an appointment to see Roosevelt. There was a good reason for the delay. The president had his hands full dealing with an escalating crisis in Europe. On September 1, 1939, German troops had invaded Poland. Within days, France and England declared war on Germany. World War II had begun. This conflict would eventually pit the Allied forces of Great Britain, France, Canada, China, the United States, and the Soviet Union against the Axis powers of Germany, Italy, and Japan.

THE URANIUM COMMITTEE

When Sachs finally met with the president on October 11, 1939, instead of just handing him Einstein's letter, Sachs made a carefully thought-out presentation to impress Roosevelt with the importance of its message. He tried to explain the recent advances in nuclear physics to Roosevelt, who knew little about science. At the same time, he made the case that the United States needed to combat the German threat by investing in atomic bomb technology. When the meeting ended, Roosevelt agreed that the U.S. government should explore the possible uses of nuclear energy. Toward that end, he established the Uranium Committee. It was composed of officials from the U.S. Army and U.S. Navy, as well as Szilard, Wigner, and Teller. Roosevelt appointed Lyman L. Briggs as the head of the committee. Briggs was the director of the National Bureau of Standards, which then oversaw the nation's physics laboratories.

The committee held its first meeting on October 21. Szilard explained that it might be possible to build a nuclear bomb with the explosive power of 20,000 tons (18,000 t) of dynamite. The military representatives found that hard to believe. Keith F.

Adamson, a lieutenant colonel with the U.S. Army, made it clear he thought the idea was completely ridiculous. He told Szilard, "In Aberdeen, [Texas], we have a goat tethered to a stick with a ten-foot rope, and we have promised a big prize to anyone who can kill the goat with a death ray. Nobody has claimed the prize yet."[3] The military men asked the scientists how much money they needed to begin their research. Unprepared for the question, Teller blurted out $6,000, an absurdly low figure. The army and navy representatives were hesitant to give them even that much.

On November 1, the committee's report on the meeting was presented to the president. It recommended exploring research into nuclear energy, but only as a "source of power in submarines."[4] Roosevelt was not particularly impressed by the report. He simply filed it, and for months, the government took no action at all.

SOLVING THE NUCLEAR PUZZLE

Even without the support of the U.S. government, research into fission and nuclear chain reactions continued. Leading physicists, however, disagreed about which element was most likely to produce nuclear energy.

Fermi was convinced that uranium-238 (U-238), the isotope of uranium most commonly found in nature, showed promise. Other scientists were investigating uranium-235 (U-235) as a fissionable material. In early 1940, John R. Dunning of Columbia and Alfred Nier at the University of Minnesota had demonstrated that they could produce fission by bombarding this isotope with slow neutrons. It was an exciting development, but it only led to more questions. In nature, there is only one part U-235 to every 140 parts U-238. Separating U-235 from the far more abundant U-238 presented a formidable challenge. Physicists studied several methods of separating and collecting U-235, but they all seemed too costly or too time consuming to work.

In Great Britain, physicists Otto Frisch and Rudolf Peierls were also studying U-235, although they were investigating the effects of bombarding it with fast-moving, rather than slow-moving, neutrons. They also turned to the question of how best to separate U-235 from U-238. They envisioned a vast industrial plant dedicated to that task. Building and operating such a plant would be hugely expensive, but by their calculations, once it was up and running, it could produce enough U-235 for a nuclear bomb in a matter of weeks. The men were exhilarated but also horrified by their discovery. Frisch had wanted to believe that building a nuclear bomb was impossible, but his research indicated the opposite was true.

Frisch and Peierls wrote up their findings in several papers. In their "Memorandum on the Properties of a Radioactive Superbomb," they explained, "the super-bomb would be practically irresistible. There is no material or structure that could be expected to resist the force of the explosion."[5] They also noted that the "super-bomb" would spread lethal radioactive material, which the wind could carry over a large region. Frisch and Peierls concluded that "the bomb could probably not be used without killing large numbers of civilians, and this may make it unsuitable as a weapon for use by this country."[6]

The Frisch-Peierls papers were sent to Henry Thomas Tizard, a noted chemist and the civilian chairman of the Committee for the Scientific Survey of Air Defence. The committee was charged with applying science to British military defense. Tizard gathered a group of physicists to study the reports. Unlike the Uranium Committee in the United States, Tizard's group took the new nuclear bomb research quite seriously.

VANNEVAR BUSH AND THE NDRC

Meanwhile, in the United States, a man named Vannevar Bush began to push the U.S. government to become more involved in nuclear research. Bush was the president of the Carnegie Institution, an organization established to support scientific research in the United States. Convinced that the United States would soon enter World War II, he also believed that the conflict "would be a highly technical struggle."[7] To win the war, America would need to employ science to create new and more devastating weapons.

With the help of Harry Hopkins, a close adviser to Roosevelt, Bush met with the president on June 12, 1940. By that time, the German army had taken over France. With anxiety growing about the escalating European war, Bush easily convinced Roosevelt to form the National Defense Research Committee (NDRC) with Bush as its head. This new group, which reported directly to the president, absorbed and reorganized the Uranium Committee.

By this time, some American physicists were also growing increasingly frustrated with the government's lack of a nuclear program. Among the most vocal was Ernest O. Lawrence, director of the Radiation Laboratory at the University of California, Berkeley. At Lawrence's insistence, Karl Compton, president of the Massachusetts Institute of Technology (MIT), wrote to Bush. Compton told Bush that British scientists were far further along in developing an atomic bomb, even though the United States now boasted "the most in number and the best in quality of nuclear physicists of the world."[8] He also warned Bush that, while the United States dawdled, the Germans were likely making progress on creating a bomb of their own.

Bush responded by assembling a committee from the National Academy of Sciences to review everything that was happening in nuclear research. Led by Karl Compton's brother Arthur, who had won the Nobel Prize in Physics in 1927, this group of eminent physicists produced a seven-page report on May 17, 1941. It concluded that scientists would soon be able to use nuclear energy to power submarines and ships and to produce deadly radioactive materials that could be scattered over enemy territory. It said, however, that it would take far longer to build an atomic bomb.

Bush was unhappy with the brief report. It did not suggest a specific plan of action or provide any concrete evidence for its conclusions. He asked the National Academy of Sciences for a second report that offered a more practical perspective. This new report, submitted on July 11, essentially endorsed the first one. Bush was again disappointed.

THE MAUD REPORT

A few days later, Bush received a draft of a third report about nuclear science. He did not commission this one, but it at last gave him the information he was looking for. The paper— called the MAUD Report—was produced by Henry Thomas Tizard's committee in England. The group took the name "MAUD" from a telegram Niels Bohr sent Otto Frisch when he was trapped in his native Denmark, which had been invaded by the Germans. The telegram referred to "Maud Ray Kent," which Frisch thought was some kind of coded message Bohr was trying to sneak out. After the war, it was revealed that Maud Ray of Kent, England, was actually a woman Bohr hired as a nanny for his children.

Drawing from the Frisch-Peierls papers, the top-secret MAUD report outlined in fairly precise terms what nuclear scientists would be able to contribute to the war effort. It also provided an estimated timetable for the creation of a bomb. The report saw two possible roads for creating an atomic bomb, with each using a different fissionable material. One bomb type would employ uranium-235. The other would use a recently discovered man-made isotope, plutonium-239. The report also said that, by the end of 1943, an industrial plant could start producing enough fissionable material to build three bombs a month. According to the MAUD report, such bombs would "lead to decisive results in the war."[9]

American officials finally had in hand a concrete plan for how to start a nuclear program. Even so, they continued to move slowly. After months of prodding from Lawrence and other physicists, Bush met with Roosevelt on October 9, 1941, to discuss the MAUD Report. Finally, the president was convinced that the United States needed to invest in nuclear research, at least to determine whether an atomic bomb was feasible. With the president's backing, the National Academy of Sciences committee submitted a third report, which estimated that a bomb would cost somewhere between $50 million and $100 million. It essentially corroborated the MAUD report, although the American committee was not quite as convinced as its British counterpart that an atomic bomb could in fact be built.

Bush brought the report to the president on November 27, 1941—more than two and a half years after Leo Szilard began sounding the alarm about the necessity of pursuing atomic bomb research. Roosevelt did not issue a response until January 19, 1942. This time, the lag was not due to inattention or disinterest. Instead, the president had far greater things on his mind. In the two months between receiving the report and responding to it, the United States had entered World War II.

The Project Begins

O n the morning of December 7, 1941, the Japanese staged a surprise attack on the U.S. naval base of Pearl Harbor on the island of Oahu, Hawaii. About 2,500 American soldiers and sailors were killed, and more than 1,000 were wounded. The following day, Congress declared war on Japan, an ally of Germany and Italy. After Germany and Italy declared war on the United States, a second declaration of war was made against those two nations on December 11.

Before Pearl Harbor, President Franklin D. Roosevelt was slow to fund efforts by scientists in the United States to build the ultimate weapon: an atomic bomb. After the attack, the situation dramatically changed. Fearing that Germany was already hard at work on an atomic bomb of its own, the president was finally willing to invest in nuclear research. Physicists could now count on government funding, but they suddenly faced a new

Before America's entry into World War II, U.S. policymakers had been slow to fund research of the development of an atomic bomb. After the Japanese sneak attack on the U.S. navy base at Pearl Harbor in Hawaii on December 7, 1941, the United States entered the war and atomic research took on a new urgency.

problem—time. They needed to create a bomb as fast at possible if their invention was to have an effect on the course of the war.

UNDER THE ARMY

Throughout the spring of 1942, nuclear research largely focused on the biggest obstacle to producing a bomb—gathering enough fissionable material to create a chain reaction. Teams of scientists were working on the problem at universities across the United States. The most notable laboratories were at Columbia

University, the University of Chicago, and the University of California, Berkeley.

To speed up these efforts, the government concluded that it needed to construct enormous industrial plants where scientists could continue their research while also using what they learned to produce fissionable material. Building these plants was a huge undertaking. Keeping them secure, so that no information about the bomb's production could reach the enemies of the United States, was also a challenge.

With an eye toward both goals, Vannevar Bush, head of the Office of Scientific Research and Development (formerly the National Defense Research Committee), asked the Army Corps of Engineers to oversee this massive project. The Corps was the federal agency in charge of building dams, roads, and other public works. Not only did the Corps have experience with large construction projects, but as part of the army, it was also able to establish the necessary military security for the proposed facilities. Giving the Corps this responsibility fundamentally changed the race to create the atomic bomb. Before, physicists and other scientists had been at the helm. Now the U.S. military would manage and direct the work of the scientific experts.

GROVES TAKES CHARGE

In the summer of 1942, Colonel James C. Marshall was placed in charge of the bomb project. He set up the Manhattan Engineer District in New York City as its headquarters. Thereafter, the U.S. program to create the atomic bomb became known as the Manhattan Project.

Unfamiliar with nuclear physics, Marshall was very cautious about moving the project forward. Bush and army officials soon agreed that they needed a bolder, more commanding leader to head the Manhattan Project. On September 17, they replaced Marshall with Colonel Leslie R. Groves, who was promoted to the rank of brigadier general six days later. Groves was an engineer who had participated in the construction of the Pentagon, the five-sided building that became the home of the U.S. Department of War in 1943.

A formidable figure with a stocky build, Groves was demanding and decisive. His close aide Kenneth D. Nichols said Groves was egotistical, abrasive, and sarcastic—"always a driver, never a praiser"—but he hailed Groves's self-confidence, intelligence, and energy. Despite the trials of working for Groves, Nichols concluded that if he "had the privilege of picking my boss, I would pick General Groves."[1]

CREATING A CHAIN REACTION

In late 1942, Groves reviewed the various methods physicists were studying for extracting uranium-235—considered the best fissionable material for a bomb—from uranium-238. No one method seemed best, so he decided to pursue several at the same time. Even though research was inconclusive, Groves determined that the Manhattan Project had to move out of the research phase and into the production and collection of U-235 as soon as possible. On December 28, 1942, Roosevelt authorized $500 million for the project, funds that would allow for the building of full-scale uranium production plants.

Earlier in the month, the bomb project also got a boost from an experiment conducted by Enrico Fermi at the University of Chicago's Metallurgical Laboratory, known as the Met Lab. In a squash court under the university's football stadium, Fermi and his team had assembled a mass of graphite blocks interlaced with rods made from uranium. Fermi called the device a pile, but it later became known as a reactor.

On December 2, 1942, an experiment involving the pile created the first controlled nuclear chain reaction. As Fermi later recalled, "The event was not spectacular, no fuses burned, no lights flashed."[2] In fact, the amount of energy released was only enough to power a flashlight. The experiment, however, had enormous implications for nuclear physics and the search

(continues on page 55)

LESLIE R. GROVES (1896–1970)

As director of the Manhattan Project, General Leslie R. Groves successfully managed the U.S. military's $2 billion program to create an atomic bomb during World War II. Groves was born on August 17, 1896, in Albany, New York. The son of an army chaplain, he and his family moved frequently. In his youth, he spent time in Cuba, China, and the Philippines.

Groves attended the University of Washington and the Massachusetts Institute of Technology before being accepted to the United States Military Academy at West Point. In 1918, he graduated fourth in his class. Groves then joined the Army Corps of Engineers and worked on construction projects in Washington, California, Hawaii, Texas, and Nicaragua. In 1922, he married Grace Wilson, with whom he had two children.

Groves joined the Office of the Chief of Engineers in Washington, D.C., in 1931. Three years later, he was promoted to captain. During the 1930s, Groves worked on projects in Nicaragua and also studied at the Command and General Staff School and the Army War College.

In preparation for the nation's possible involvement in World War II, the U.S. Army began building new military training bases and other facilities. As deputy chief of construction, Groves oversaw much of this expansion. He also supervised the construction of the Pentagon, which became the headquarters of the U.S. Department of War. Groves was promoted to lieutenant colonel in 1941.

In 1942, Vannevar Bush, chairman of the Office of Scientific Research and Development, was looking for a new director for the Manhattan Project, the military's program for developing a nuclear weapon. Two generals suggested

Major General Leslie R. Groves was the military commander of the Manhattan Project, which developed the atomic bomb during World War II. Groves predicted that two atomic bombs would stun Japan into surrender and end the war.

Groves. By then, he had gained a reputation in the Corps as a manager who knew how to cut through government

(continues)

(continued)

bureaucracy and get complicated and expensive projects done. He was also well known for his arrogance and abrasiveness. Although Bush was concerned about Groves's temperament, he was persuaded to hire him to head the Manhattan Project.

Groves immediately began scouting for locations for plants to produce the uranium and plutonium needed to create atomic weapons. At Oak Ridge, Tennessee, and Hanford, Washington, he oversaw not only the construction of these enormous production facilities but also brand new towns around them. Groves also directed the building of a laboratory in the remote community of Los Alamos, New Mexico. There, scientists from universities across the country came to live as they worked together to create the atomic bomb.

Groves's hard-driving style repelled some of the Los Alamos scientists. Groves, however, developed an extremely close and effective working relationship with J. Robert Oppenheimer, the director of scientific research at Los Alamos. The trust and cooperation between these two men were central to the success of the Manhattan Project.

After the war, Groves was a strong advocate for maintaining military control over the nation's nuclear weapons program. Despite his efforts, the program was placed under the jurisdiction of the civilian-operated Atomic Energy Commission in 1947. Groves left the army and joined the Sperry Rand Corporation as a vice president of research and development. There, Groves oversaw the creation of UNIVAC, one of the first commercially available computers. After his retirement in 1961, he published *Now It Can Be Told* (1962), his memoir of working on the Manhattan Project. On July 13, 1970, Groves died of heart failure. He was buried with military honors in Arlington National Cemetery near Washington, D.C.

(continued from page 51)

for the atomic bomb. Fermi's work convinced many previously skeptical scientists that the bomb could be built after all. Hans Bethe, for instance, had believed that "trying to make [an atomic bomb] was a waste of time" until Fermi showed that a chain reaction and a resulting energy release was possible. "[F]rom that moment on," Bethe noted, "I was fairly confident that one way or another, a weapon would be made."[3]

OAK RIDGE

In late 1942, Groves chose a site in eastern Tennessee for his uranium operation. The site had several things to recommend it. Few people lived in this rural area, but it was readily accessible by car and train. The region had a mild climate that would facilitate year-round work. It was also near the Clinch River, which could provide hydroelectric power to run the plants Groves envisioned.

The army bought or confiscated about 59,000 acres (23,876 hectares) in the area and began construction of the Clinton Engineering Works. They also built roads and dwellings to accommodate a large workforce. Initially, they expected this makeshift town to have a population of about 13,000. By the summer of 1943, however, the town that later became known as Oak Ridge was home to about 45,000 residents.

For security purposes, the army kept Oak Ridge laborers in the dark about the bomb project. Most, however, did not care what they were working on. They were simply happy to earn paychecks far bigger than they could have in nearby farming communities. As many young men had joined the military, a large number of workers at Oak Ridge were women. There were also many African-American laborers, because the government forbade the army from discriminating against nonwhite workers at the facility. In keeping with the legal and cultural norms of the American South at the time, however, black workers were not allowed to socialize with or live in the same areas as white

A photo of Oak Ridge, Tennessee, as it looked on April 21, 1959. When it was first founded in 1942 to supply housing for workers at the Atomic Energy Commission plant, Oak Ridge was a military reservation with a fence and armed guards. It was incorporated as a civilian city in 1959.

workers. African-American workers generally had to live in the worst housing available.

URANIUM-235 AND PLUTONIUM

Two plants at Oak Ridge had the same goal—to separate the rare uranium isotope U-235 from the more common form of uranium, U-238. The facilities, however, used different means to collect the precious U-235. At a building code-named K-25, workers employed a method called gaseous diffusion. By this technique, U-238 was converted to a gas and then pumped through thousands of barriers with millions of extremely tiny holes. Because atoms of U-235 were lighter than atoms of U-238, they passed through the barriers faster, allowing scientists to separate the rare U-235 atoms within the gaseous U-238.

In a building called Y-12, this separation was achieved through the electromagnetic method. Here, uranium gas was given an electric charge and sent through a magnetic field created by a 4,900-ton (4,445 t) magnet. Again because they were lighter, the U-235 atoms would follow a different arc in this magnetic field than the U-238 atoms in the gas.

The army began construction of a third plant at Oak Ridge called X-10. Instead of collecting U-235, it was to produce another fissionable material: the man-made radioactive element plutonium. After a few months, however, Groves decided against the plan. X-10 would require more energy to operate than was available at Oak Ridge. Its location about 25 miles (40 km) from the city of Knoxville, Tennessee, was also a problem. Groves feared that an accident at the plant could expose the city's population to deadly plutonium radiation.

For that reason, Groves found an isolated site thousands of miles away for the plutonium plant. It was located near the town of Hanford in southeastern Washington state, near the Columbia River. Groves contracted the DuPont Company to enlarge the town and build a facility there called the Hanford Engineer Works. In just two years, Hanford was transformed from a sparsely populated area, covered with sheep-grazing lands and fruit farms, to the fourth-largest city in Washington.

Finding workers from outside the region was necessary because the population was originally so small. Recruiting from far and wide, the facility attracted mostly single male workers. Like western gold-rush towns of the nineteenth century, Hanford was a rough and violent place. According to physicist Leona Marshall, "There was nothing to do after work except fight, with the result that occasionally bodies were found in garbage cans the next morning."[4]

THE LOS ALAMOS LABORATORY

Groves decided that the Manhattan Project needed a third facility, one that would bring together in one place all the best theoretical and experimental scientists and mathematicians engaged in nuclear research. Years later, Oppenheimer recounted how he discussed the idea with Groves at their first meeting in October 1942:

> I became convinced, as did others, that a major change was called for in the work on the bomb itself. We needed a central laboratory devoted wholly to this purpose, where people could talk freely with each other, where theoretical ideas and experimental findings could affect each other, where the waste and frustration and error of the many compartmentalized experimental studies could be eliminated, where we could begin to come to grips with chemical, metallurgical, engineering, and ordnance problems that had so far received no consideration.[5]

Security was Groves's primary concern in scouting a location for this facility. If the scientists there were permitted to exchange ideas freely, it was important that none of their discussions could be leaked to the world outside. The site, therefore, had to be relatively unpopulated and isolated, so that people would not be able to move in or out of the facility without being sighted by military guards. Oppenheimer suggested a site in New Mexico, where he owned a ranch. Groves considered the Jemez Springs area, but rejected it because it had no good roads. Instead, he chose Los Alamos, a community located on a 7,000-foot-high (2,000-meter-high) mesa in the north-central part of the state. Largely a grazing area for ranches, Los Alamos was also home to an exclusive private school for boys. The army purchased the school and about 54,000 acres (21,853 ha) surrounding it and began constructing a research facility there in early 1943.

OPPENHEIMER AS SCIENTIFIC DIRECTOR

Groves selected Oppenheimer to serve as Los Alamos's scientific director. The choice was odd for a number of reasons. Personally and physically, the two men were opposites. The heavyset Groves was a brusque, disciplined military man, always focused on practical matters. The tall and thin Oppenheimer had a sensitive, philosophical nature, which excited his interest in poetry and religion as well as science. Oppenheimer also had little management experience and had once had ties to the Communist Party, which the U.S. military viewed with suspicion. In addition, although Oppenheimer had never won the Nobel Prize, he would be overseeing of the work of several Nobel Prize winners, who might question his authority over them. Despite these facts, Groves had great confidence in Oppenheimer. "He's a genius," Groves later said, "A real genius. . . . Why, Oppenheimer knows about everything."[6]

Oppenheimer's first job was persuading the best scientists in the United States to stop their research, pack their bags, and come to a remote area in New Mexico to live and work for the duration of the war. Oppenheimer traveled to all corners of the country, asking scholars to give up their comfortable academic surroundings to work for the U.S. government. "The notion of disappearing into the desert for an indeterminate period and under quasi-military auspices disturbed a good many scientists and the families of many more,"[7] he later recalled. In the end, however, most took him up on his offer. Oppenheimer later explained:

> Almost everyone realized that this was a great undertaking. Almost everyone knew that if it were completed successfully and rapidly enough, it might determine the outcome of

the war. Almost everyone knew that it was an unparalleled opportunity to bring to bear the basic knowledge and art of science for the benefit of his country. Almost everyone knew that this job, if it were achieved, would be part of history. This sense of excitement, of devotion and of patriotism in the end prevailed.[8]

Life at Los Alamos

On March 15, 1943, Oppenheimer arrived in Santa Fe, New Mexico, and waited for his anxious recruits to arrive. Over the next four weeks, many of the world's greatest scientists, traveling with their families by car and by train, made their way to the historic desert town. They had instructions to report to 109 East Palace Street, where they were given badges to admit them to Los Alamos, located about 45 miles (72 km) to the southwest.

Upon arriving in Los Alamos, the recruits quickly learned they would have to be careful about what they said. Security details insisted that no one ever use the words *physicist* or *chemist* to make sure nothing about the secret facility leaked out to the public. Instead, the scientists developed their own code, calling physicists "fizzlers" and chemists "stinkers." Some famous scientists were even given new names to protect their identities. Enrico Fermi, for instance, became known as Mr. Farmer.

New arrivals in Los Alamos were often put off by their first look at the place. Like Oak Ridge and Hanford, Los Alamos was a community that had been thrown together virtually overnight. While the stone and log buildings that remained from the town's old boarding school provided comfortable homes and meeting areas, the rest of the town was made up of hastily built houses, barracks, and trailers, all lining dusty dirt roads. For many, the most disturbing thing about Los Alamos was the barbed wire fence that surrounded it. Armed soldiers patrolled the fence around the clock. Many European refugees among the recruits looked at the fence and shuddered—it reminded them of Hitler's concentration camps in Germany.

A STRANGE NEW WORLD

The newcomers quickly tried to make the best of their strange surroundings. They got used to dealing with housing shortages, crowded laundries, and continual problems with the water supply. They also became accustomed to having their letters to relatives and friends read and censored by army officials afraid of security leaks.

At Los Alamos, parents had to struggle to give their children a sense of normalcy while they were confined in what was essentially a military compound. With most of the adults in their twenties and thirties, the town was full of families with young children. During the Manhattan Project, some 330 babies were born in Los Alamos. The security was so great that the town's name did not appear on their birth certificates. Instead, the cryptic "P.O. Box 1663" was listed as the babies' place of birth.

Security concerns also created a peculiar dynamic within families. The scientists, almost all men, spent 10 to 12 hours a day working before returning home exhausted night after night. Their wives knew they were working hard on something important, but the scientists were forbidden from telling their families any details about what they were doing. The women of Los Alamos found themselves living in an odd place surrounded by guards and had no idea why. Sharing this peculiar and intense experience, many became unusually close. One wife later recalled, "When one considers that we lived . . . closely packed together—aware of every detail of our neighbors' lives—even what they were having for dinner every night—one can't help but marvel that we enjoyed each other so much."[1]

That camaraderie was especially evident on the weekends. Saturday nights were the time when everyone in Los Alamos took a few hours to blow off steam. As Bernice Brode, wife of Robert Brode, later wrote, "Parties, both big and brassy and small and cheerful, were an integral part of mesa life. It was a poor Saturday night that some large affair was not scheduled, and there were usually several of them."[2] Fuller Hall, a large old school building, became a site for weekly square dances. Dressed in jeans and boots, the Los Alamos scientists, many from Europe, pretended they were Southwestern natives. On Sundays, they took the day off to relax and enjoy the beautiful landscape of the region. Oppenheimer rode horses, Segré and Fermi took up fishing, and Bethe went mountain climbing. Kistiakowsky used his leisure time to teach his fellow theoreticians how to play poker, although he complained that once their agile minds mastered the rules of the game, he had trouble winning the pot.

The world of Los Alamos was somewhat grimmer for less prestigious workers. Beginning in October 1943, army soldiers with machinist skills or science backgrounds were assigned to the Special Engineer Detachment (SED) to serve as support staff. While the scientists got the best housing, they had to live in army barracks. For much of their tenure, SED soldiers were expected to start the day with morning calisthenics and endure Saturday morning inspections. They often felt the scientists

(continues on page 66)

J. ROBERT OPPENHEIMER (1904–1967)

J. Robert Oppenheimer is often referred to as the "father of the atomic bomb" because of his crucial role in the Manhattan Project. Oppenheimer was born on April 22, 1904, in New York City. Early on, his wealthy, cultured parents recognized his intellectual gifts. After graduating from New York's Ethical Culture School, he studied chemistry and physics at Harvard University in 1922. Earning his undergraduate degree in just three years, Oppenheimer then moved to Europe to pursue his interest in theoretical physics with noted physicists Max Born and Wolfgang Pauli.

After earning his doctorate, Oppenheimer returned to the United States. He was hired as a professor at the University of California, Berkeley, one of the leading American centers for nuclear research. Oppenheimer earned a reputation as a challenging and inspirational teacher as well as a brilliant physicist.

In early 1942, Oppenheimer was asked to serve as the director of the U.S. government's research laboratory at Los Alamos, New Mexico. He and his staff were charged with creating a nuclear bomb during World War II. Oppenheimer relentlessly pursued this goal, all the while keeping his scientists focused and motivated. His intellect and leadership were instrumental to their success.

In the final days of World War II, Oppenheimer, as part of a scientific panel formed to advise the president, endorsed the U.S. military's use of the atomic bomb against Japan. After the war, however, he helped author the Acheson-Lilienthal Report, which recommended controls on atomic weapons to prevent an international arms race. In the 1950s, Oppenheimer became a prominent opponent of the development of the hydrogen bomb, a weapon 500 times

J. Robert Oppenheimer is shown in front of a blackboard on December 17, 1947, shortly after his appointment to the director-ship of the Institute for Advanced Study at Princeton University. Oppenheimer was the scientific director of the Manhattan Project.

more powerful than the atomic bombs the United States had dropped on the Japanese cities of Hiroshima and Nagasaki.

Because of his stance against the hydrogen bomb and because of his past affiliation with the Communist Party, Oppenheimer was accused of being an agent of the USSR. After a congressional hearing, he was found to be a loyal citizen but nevertheless was stripped of his security clear-ance. Although embittered by the experience, Oppenheimer continued to speak out about politics and to lecture on physics around the world. In 1963, he received the presti-gious Enrico Fermi Award.

Between 1947 and 1966, Oppenheimer was the direc-tor of the Institute for Advanced Study in Princeton, New Jersey. He died of throat cancer at his home in Princeton on February 18, 1967.

(continued from page 63)
they worked with did not respect them and resented that the scientists did not have to follow military rules as they did.

INFORMATION AND IDEAS

When establishing Los Alamos, Groves had wanted to make the participating scientists commissioned army officers, which would have subjected them to army protocol. The scientists, however, resisted. The purpose of Los Alamos was to speed the creation of the atomic bomb by allowing the scientists there to share their knowledge and to discuss new theories freely. They sensed that a strict military hierarchy among the personnel was likely to inhibit the free flow of information and ideas.

The creation of Los Alamos also challenged one of Groves's guiding principles for the Manhattan Project: the compartmentalizing of knowledge. For security's sake, Groves had tried to have scientists working on the bomb focus only on their own research. In this way, no one person could know too much about the project as a whole, making it more difficult for vital information about the bomb program to leak out.

At Los Alamos, however, the scientists involved in the Manhattan Project were largely segregated from the outside world, secured within their fenced-in town. In this environment, even Groves felt it was safe for them to learn about their colleagues' work. To bring the new recruits up to speed about the latest nuclear research, physicist Robert Serber delivered a series of five brief lectures at Los Alamos in April 1943. Notes from these talks were compiled into the *Los Alamos Primer*, which thereafter all scientific experts were expected to read as soon as they arrived in town.

THE QUEBEC AGREEMENT

The most important later recruits to the project were 19 prominent scientists who had been living in England. They included such luminaries as James Chadwick, Rudolf Peierls, and Otto Frisch. This British contingent arrived in Los Alamos in late 1943 after the United States and Great Britain signed the Quebec Agreement. In this agreement, President Franklin Roosevelt and Prime Minister Winston Churchill of Great Britain pledged that their two nations would collaborate on building the bomb. The British would submit their research to the Americans, who in turn would provide regular updates on the project. The contribution of British scientists proved substantial, especially in terms of theoretical research. Bethe, Los Alamos's head theoretician, later said the collaboration was absolutely essential to the success of the Manhattan Project.

Perhaps the most important scientist sent to Los Alamos from England was Niels Bohr. A revered figure in the world of physics, he helped build morale with his very presence. As Oppenheimer explained, "Bohr at Los Alamos was marvelous. He took a very lively technical interest. . . . But his real function, I think for almost all of us, was not the technical one. He made the enterprise seem hopeful, when many were not free of misgiving."[3] Many scientists at Los Alamos were not only frustrated by the unrelenting pressure they were under to solve the mysteries of nuclear energy; they were also disturbed by the idea that, if they succeeded, they would be responsible for creating the most devastating weapon the world had ever known. Bohr and Oppenheimer tried to ease their concerns. They promoted the optimistic view that, by building the atomic bomb, they were helping to end war for all time. The bomb and the destruction it threatened to cause, they reasoned, would force nations to find new ways of solving conflicts.

DESIGNING THE GADGET

At Los Alamos, scientists worked hard to understand a variety of questions. What were the properties of uranium and plutonium? How much fissionable material was needed to create a chain reaction? What was the best method for converting gaseous uranium and plutonium to metal and shaping its solid form for use in the bomb?

This is the "Fat Man" atomic bomb, the type that was detonated over Nagasaki, Japan, during World War II. The weapon was 60 inches (1.5 m) in diameter and 128 inches (3.25 m) long. The second nuclear weapon to be detonated, it weighed about 10,000 pounds (4,500 kilograms) and had a yield equivalent of approximately 20,000 tons (18,000 t) of TNT.

Just as crucial was determining the best design for the bomb, or the Gadget, as the scientists called it. The earliest bomb models worked on gun technology. These gun-method bombs shot one mass of fissionable material at another mass at high speed. The collision was supposed to produce a nuclear chain reaction resulting in a massive explosion.

By early 1944, bomb designers had created two gun models. Thin Man, named in honor of Roosevelt, used plutonium. The smaller and lighter Little Boy employed uranium-235. The mood at Los Alamos lightened as the scientists finally felt close to achieving their goal. That confidence, however, was suddenly dashed when Emilio Segré discovered that the Thin Man design was hopelessly flawed. He found that unless the plutonium used was absolutely pure, Thin Man would fail to create the desired explosion. This news was an enormous setback. The Los Alamos scientists were already worried about getting enough uranium from Oak Ridge to power Little Boy. (The Y-12 electromagnetic facility was just up and running, and the K-25 gaseous diffusion plant was underperforming because of inadequate barrier material.) Now, with the failure of Thin Man, it seemed unlikely they would have a working atomic bomb anytime in the near future. During the summer of 1944, the entire Manhattan Project, which was now costing the U.S. government $100 million per month, appeared in jeopardy.

THE IMPLOSION BOMB

Out of desperation, the Los Alamos scientists began exploring another bomb model based on implosion technology devised by physicist Seth Neddermeyer and mathematician John von Neumann. The implosion bomb was composed of a sphere of plutonium surrounded by conventional explosives. When they were detonated, the explosives squeezed the plutonium so tight that it set off a nuclear chain reaction. The scientists called the new bomb Fat Man, in tribute to Churchill.

In the summer of 1944, the Manhattan Project looked poised for failure. By early 1945, however, its prospects appeared far brighter. Field tests had confirmed that Little Boy, the uranium gun bomb, would be workable and ready for use by August 1, 1945. Oppenheimer's decision to redirect resources and manpower to Fat Man, the plutonium implosion bomb, also seemed to be paying off. In February 1945, Los Alamos had a final design for Little Boy, and the next month, the design for Fat Man was approved. Just as important, the Oak Ridge and Hanford plants were at last on track. They began delivering fissionable material to Los Alamos in the spring of 1945.

This is the "Little Boy" atomic bomb, the type that was detonated over Hiroshima, Japan, during World War II. The weapon was 29 inches (74 centimeters) in diameter and 126 inches (3.2 m) long. The first nuclear weapon to be detonated in wartime, it weighed 9,700 pounds (4,400 kg) and had a yield equivalent of approximately 20,000 tons (18,000 t) of TNT.

READYING FOR TRINITY

Oppenheimer decided not to test Little Boy. The scientists at Los Alamos were fairly confident in its design. Besides, they could not afford to waste precious uranium-235 on a test. Oppenheimer, however, was not so sure about Fat Man. To find out whether the implosion bomb would really work, he organized the top-secret Trinity test, which was scheduled to take place in the summer.

Before Trinity, two events happened that changed the course of the Manhattan Project. On April 12, 1945, Roosevelt suffered a cerebral hemorrhage and died. The army, and hence the Manhattan Project, were suddenly under the command of a new president, Harry S. Truman, who as vice president had known almost nothing about the atomic bomb program.

Then, on May 8, 1945, Germany surrendered to the United States and its allies, ending the war in Europe. (Italy had surrendered in September 1943.) The Manhattan Project, originally envisioned as a program to beat Germany to the bomb, in the end had no impact on the war with Germany. The United States, however, was still at war with Japan. It would be up to the new commander in chief to determine what role the bomb would play in the final days of World War II.

Bombing Japan

When Harry S. Truman assumed the presidency, the Japanese were facing defeat. The U.S. Air Force had subjected their capital, Tokyo, to a series of fire bombings. During just one air raid, as many as 100,000 Japanese were killed. U.S. Navy ships had also surrounded the islands of Japan. They were blocking food and supplies from reaching the Japanese people, as well as the nation's military.

Despite Japan's dire situation, American officials believed that the Japanese would fight as long as they possibly could. As a result, the Americans expected that the only thing that could force Japan to accept defeat was an all-out invasion of the islands by the Allied forces. Such an invasion would be enormously costly—not just in money, but also in lives. One estimate put the loss in American lives at one million; in all of

World War II, 418,500 Americans were killed. Japanese casualties were estimated in the millions.

The news from Los Alamos, however, presented Truman with an alternative to invading Japan. Perhaps the atomic bomb could persuade even the most intractable Japanese leaders to give up the fight.

THE INTERIM COMMITTEE

With Truman's approval, Secretary of War Henry L. Stimson organized the Interim Committee in May 1945 to discuss the matter. The committee included leading figures from the military, business, and scientific communities. Two of the most prominent members were Vannevar Bush and James F. Byrnes, a U.S. senator who would soon become Truman's secretary of state.

The top-secret Interim Committee was charged with deciding how the atomic bomb should be used in the war against Japan. In addition, it considered what role the bomb would play in postwar policy. The United States and the USSR were allies in the war, but the president did not trust Joseph Stalin, the autocratic Soviet leader. Therefore, many in the U.S. government believed the atomic bomb was potentially a tool not only for forcing a Japanese surrender but also for controlling the Soviets' behavior after the war's end.

Four science advisers assisted the Interim Committee: J. Robert Oppenheimer, Enrico Fermi, Arthur Compton, and Ernest O. Lawrence. They came together at Los Alamos to discuss what recommendations they would make to the committee. The four scientists considered suggesting that the United States drop the bomb on an unpopulated island as a warning to the Japanese but ultimately rejected the idea. "[W]e can propose no technical demonstration likely to bring an end to the war; we see no acceptable alternative to direct military use," they wrote in their report to the Interim Committee.[1]

The committee members agreed. They believed that a mere demonstration would not be enough to impress the Japanese. They thought the Japanese would be persuaded to surrender only by the shock value of mass destruction. Such an action would also send a message to the Soviets, whom the committee believed did not have the production facilities to produce their own atomic weapons for years to come.

The Interim Committee determined that the United States should drop bombs on one or more Japanese cities. It came up with four targets: Kokura, Hiroshima, Niigata, and Kyoto. Stimson, however, spoke out against bombing Kyoto, because it was a great Japanese cultural center. The group agreed and replaced it with the city of Nagasaki.

THE FRANCK REPORT

Although they had long been aware of the fact they were making a bomb, some Manhattan Project scientists were appalled by the idea that their invention would be used against the Japanese. In June 1945, a group at the Met Lab at the University of Chicago met in secret at night to draft their own argument against using the bomb. The group produced the Franck Report, which was named after its chairman, James Franck. With their eyes on the postwar balance of power, they suggested a demonstration of the bomb as a way of forcing the international community to adopt controls for the future use of the atomic bomb by any country. The Franck Report also warned that if the bomb were dropped on Japan, it would set off a disastrous worldwide arms race, in which all powerful nations would frantically set up their own nuclear programs to make sure they had the bomb before their enemies did. The Franck Report was delivered to policymakers in Washington, D.C., but it had little influence. The Interim Committee ignored the concerns of the Met Lab scientists, preferring instead the advice of its science advisers, who supported bombing Japan.

In early July, Leo Szilard, who signed the Franck Report, began circulating a petition to the president. It declared that it would be wrong for the United States to be the first country to unleash the bomb on an enemy. His petition stated, "[A] nation which sets the precedent of using these newly liberated forces of nature for purposes of destruction may have to bear the responsibility of opening the door to an era of devastation on an unimaginable scale."[2]

Edward Teller, after talking it over with Oppenheimer, refused to sign Szilard's petition. As Teller explained, "The things we are working on are so terrible that no amount of protesting or fiddling with politics will save our souls."[3] He held that bombing Japan would convince the world never to use an atomic bomb again: "Our only hope is in getting the facts of our results before the people. This might help to convince everybody that the next war would be fatal. For this purpose actual combat-use might be the best thing."[4]

THE POTSDAM CONFERENCE

In mid-July, Truman traveled to Germany to meet with Prime Minister Churchill and Premier Stalin in the city of Potsdam, where they were to discuss what actions the Allies should take to end the war in Japan. Accepting the recommendations of the Interim Committee, Truman had already made up his mind to use the atomic bomb against the Japanese—that is, if the atomic bomb actually worked. He was still awaiting word from Los Alamos about the outcome of the Trinity test.

On July 16, Truman and Secretary of State James F. Byrnes were touring Berlin, Germany's war-ravaged capital. Stimson, the secretary of war, was already in Potsdam preparing for the conference. There, he received a cable from Washington, D.C., from his assistant, George L. Harrison: "Operated on this morning. Diagnosis not yet complete but results seem satisfactory and already exceed expectations. Local press

From left, Premier Joseph Stalin of the Soviet Union, President Harry Truman of the United States, Prime Minister Winston Churchill of Great Britain, and their interpreters engage in informal conversation just prior to the opening of the Potsdam Conference in Germany on July 17, 1945.

release necessary as interest extends great distance. Dr. Groves pleased. He returns tomorrow. I will keep you posted."[5]

Stimson immediately understood Harrison's carefully coded message. The "operation" Harrison wrote of was actually the Trinity test. Stimson was greatly relieved to hear it had exceeded expectations and that Groves was pleased with the results. After all, Stimson had pushed for the government's funding of the Manhattan Project, which eventually totaled about $2 billion. After reading the cable, he joked that now he no longer had to fear the military throwing him in prison for wasting a fortune of taxpayers' money. When Truman and Churchill reached Potsdam, Stimson shared the news with the two leaders, who were equally relieved.

NEWS FROM LOS ALAMOS

After the Potsdam Conference began, Stimson continued to receive encouraging information about Trinity. On July 21, he read to Truman a long report from Groves, which included eyewitness accounts of the blast. According to Groves, the scientists at Los Alamos had determined that the explosion was the equivalent of one produced by 15,000 to 20,000 tons (13,600 to 18,000 t) of TNT. Stimson later recalled that Truman was "tremendously pepped up" by the report.[6] It not only suggested that the United States might be able to win the war without invading Japan, but also gave Truman the upper hand in his dealings with Stalin.

On July 24, Stimson told Truman that Little Boy, the uranium bomb, would be ready to drop sometime between August 1 and August 10. Fat Man, the plutonium bomb, would likely be ready by August 6. Armed with this knowledge, Truman decided to mention the bomb to Stalin, who had previously been kept out of all discussions about the Manhattan Project. That evening, without an interpreter present, Truman told the Soviet premier that the United States had a new and incredibly powerful weapon. Stalin took in the news without emotion. According to Truman, he casually responded by saying he hoped the president would make "good use of it against the Japanese."[7] Stalin's cool demeanor was not just a pose. He was genuinely unsurprised by the news because he already knew about the atomic bomb from Soviet spies. Among them was Klaus Fuchs, a Los Alamos scientist from the British contingent who had been passing information to the Soviets.

The result of the conference was the Potsdam Declaration, which was issued on July 26. It threatened that if Japan did not surrender unconditionally, it would face "prompt and utter destruction."[8] Although many Japanese were eager to end the war, the Japanese government responded three days later by refusing to surrender.

ON TINIAN ISLAND

Even before this disappointing response, the U.S. military had put in motion its plans for an atomic bomb attack on Japan. The 509th Composite Group received orders to "deliver its first special bomb as soon as weather will permit visual bombing after about 3 August 1945 on one of the [four chosen] targets."[9] This air combat unit had been organized in December 1944 under the command of Colonel Paul W. Tibbets. His men had begun their training at a secluded base in Wendover, Utah. In May 1945, they had relocated to Tinian, one of the Northern Marianas islands in the Pacific, where the air force built the largest air base in the world.

The members of the 509th Composite Group noticed that Tinian was shaped a little like New York City's Manhattan Island, where the Manhattan Project had first began. They named the roads they built on Tinian after Manhattan's famous streets. While preparing for the atomic bomb drop, the airmen on Tinian traveled down Wall Street and Broadway, occasionally passing a livestock reserve they nicknamed Central Park.

Throughout the summer, flight crews practiced flying B-29 bombers specially equipped to hold and release atomic weapons. They went on dozens of missions over Japan dropping "pumpkins"—bombs the size and shape of Fat Man but filled with conventional explosives.

PREPARING LITTLE BOY

Shipped from the United States and assembled on Tinian, Little Boy was ready for use by August 1. Two days later, Tibbets and William "Deke" Parsons, the bomb commander, briefed the flight crews that would fly the first atomic bomb mission. Parsons told them that they were going to drop the most destructive weapon ever produced in the history of the world. Before the briefing, none of the airmen knew anything about the atomic bomb. They were disturbed and stunned by what they heard. In his diary, one of the men, Sergeant Abe Spitzer, wrote, "It is like some weird dream conceived by one with too vivid an imagination."[10]

After a few days of bad weather, Tibbets and his crews prepared for their mission in the early hours of August 6, 1945. Their target was to be Hiroshima; it was selected from the four possible candidates because it supposedly did not house any American prisoners of war. (In fact, about 20 American POWs were in the city at the time.) Around midnight, the men ate a hearty breakfast of ham and eggs. They then posed for photographs. Tibbets was to fly the plane that would drop Little Boy. He found a former sign painter on Tinian and had him paint his mother's name—*Enola Gay*—on the side of the plane. American airmen often painted pinup girls on their planes, but Tibbets wanted to honor his mother because she had always supported his decision to become a pilot. Some airmen signed their names on the bomb. A few wrote obscene messages taunting the Japanese enemy.

At about 2:30 A.M., the *Enola Gay* took off from Tinian and headed north toward Japan. On board was Little Boy, which weighed almost 10,000 pounds (4,500 kg). In the bomb bay, two men worked on its final assembly during the 1,500-mile (2,400-km) trip to Hiroshima.

DROPPING THE BOMB

As they neared the city, the plane's crew put on flak jackets in case Japanese planes fired on them, but there were no enemy fighter planes in sight. Tibbets also reminded his men to put on special dark goggles. The goggles were supposed to protect their eyes from the light emitted when the bomb exploded.

At 8:15, when they were directly above the city, the crew of the *Enola Gay* dropped the bomb. An expert pilot, Tibbets

The ground crew of the B-29 bomber *Enola Gay*, which dropped the Little Boy atomic bomb on Hiroshima, Japan, on August 6, 1945, stands with pilot Colonel Paul W. Tibbets *(center)* in the Marianas Islands.

then made a sharp 155-degree turn, tearing the plane through the sky and speeding away from the explosion's reach. The crew had been told that it would take 43 seconds to explode. As the seconds ticked away, they started to wonder whether this weapon, supposedly the most deadly ever, was nothing more than a dud.

When the *Enola Gay* was 11 miles (17.6 km) from Hiroshima, the plane was suddenly rocked by a massive shockwave. Two more followed, then the airmen saw a bright flash. Tibbets circled the plane around so the men could get a sense of the damage. When they looked down, they saw nothing but smoke and fire where there had been a city of 300,000 just moments before. Tibbets later described the site:

> It was a very sobering event, as we turned back over the target to take camera photos of the area. A boiling, tumbling, rolling cloud rose up from the ground. The cloud went up rapidly and was 10,000 feet [3,048 m] above us and climbing by the time we had turned around. Down below all you could see was a black, boiling nest.[11]

Theodore J. Van Kirk, the *Enola Gay*'s navigator, remembered looking at the remains of Hiroshima and being overwhelmed by a single thought: "Thank God the war is over and I don't have to get shot at any more. I can go home."[12]

ATTACK ON HIROSHIMA

It had been a beautiful morning in Hiroshima. The sky was clear, and the air was warm and humid, promising a steamy, sunny day. People left home for work, and children rushed off to school. Soldiers at an army base lined up, ready to perform their rigorous morning calisthenics.

Then, Little Boy exploded about 1,900 feet (580 m) above the city. Within a fraction of a second, the temperature at ground zero reached 5,400° Fahrenheit (3,000° Celsius). The blast killed about 70,000 people instantly. Human beings on the ground were transformed into small piles of black char, stuck to the sidewalks and streets that just a moment before had been crowded with people busily going about their morning routine.

Many of the survivors were left to die an agonizing death. Their skin was so burnt that their flesh was peeling off their bodies. One man who lived through the day described the horrible plight of the dying:

The appearance of people was . . . well, they all had skin blackened by burns. . . . They had no hair because their hair was burned, and at a glance you couldn't tell whether you were looking at them from in front or in back. . . . They held their arms [in front of them] . . . and their skin—not

CHILDREN OF THE A-BOMB

Japanese educator Arata Osada asked a group of children who survived the atomic bombing of Hiroshima on August 6, 1945, to write compositions about their experiences. Compiled in his book *Children of the A-Bomb* (1963), these accounts create a chilling picture of the horrors experienced by Japanese civilians in the aftermath of Little Boy's deadly blast. The following are some excerpts:

The blast: "Ah, that instant! I felt as though I had been struck on the back with something like a big hammer, and thrown into boiling oil."

The destroyed city: "When I opened my eyes after being thrown at least eight yards, . . . [t]he first thing that my eyes lighted upon then was the flat stretch of land with only dust clouds rising from it. Everything had crumbled away in that one moment, and changed into streets of rubble, street after street of ruins."

The incinerated bodies: "A streetcar was all burned and just the skeleton of it was left, and inside it all the passengers were burned to a cinder. When I saw that I shuddered all over and started to tremble."

The burn victims: "The people passing along the street are covered with blood and trailing the rags of their torn clothes after them. The skin of their arms is peeled off and dangling from their finger tips, and they go walking silently, hanging their arms before them."

only on their hands, but on their faces and bodies too—hung down.[13]

Hiroshima itself was utterly destroyed. Almost all of its buildings were reduced to rubble. Because of the heat of the

---

The suffering elderly: "The flames which blaze up here and there from the collapsed houses as though to illuminate the darkness. . . . The old man, the skin of his face and body peeling off like a potato skin, mumbling prayers while he flees with faltering steps. . . . This is the way war really looks."

The horrifically injured: "There was . . . a person who had a big splinter of wood stuck in his eye—I suppose maybe he couldn't see—and he was running around blindly."

The search for loved ones: "Screaming children who have lost sight of their mothers; voices of mothers searching for their little ones; people who can no longer bear the heat, cooling their bodies in cisterns; every one among the fleeing people is dyed red with blood."

The spreading fires: "The whole city . . . was burning. Black smoke was billowing up and we could hear the sound of big things exploding. . . . Those dreadful streets. The fires were burning. There was a strange smell all over. Blue-green balls of fire were drifting around. I had a terrible lonely feeling that everybody else in the world was dead and only we were still alive."

The escape from Hiroshima: "On that street crowds were fleeing toward the west. . . . Along the way the road was full to overflowing with victims, some with great wounds, some burned, and some who had lost the strength to move farther."*

---

* Richard Rhodes, *The Making of the Atomic Bomb*. New York: Simon & Schuster, 1986, pp. 716-722.

A photo of of Hiroshima, Japan, following the atomic bombing of August 6, 1945. At center, the building now known as "the atomic dome," which today houses the Hiroshima Peace Memorial. More than 70,000 people were killed instantly by the bomb blast. By 1950, another 13,000 had suffered fatal injuries from the radiation.

blast, everything left was soon engulfed in flames. Any survivor pinned in the wreckage or too injured to escape burned to death as the fires raged.

Even people far from ground zero were not spared. In the weeks to come, survivors started coming down with a strange and violent illness. They became nauseous and vomited. They developed fevers and grew weak with diarrhea. Purple spots appeared on their skin, and their mouths and throats became inflamed. For many, the symptoms continued to worsen until they finally died. Doctors eventually realized these people were suffering painful deaths from exposure to radiation released by the bomb. Because of radiation sickness, the people of Hiroshima continued to die long after the initial blast. By the end of 1945, 140,000 were dead. Five years later, the death toll had risen to 200,000.

WINNING THE BATTLE OF THE LABORATORIES

On August 6, Truman was on a navy ship. With the Potsdam Conference over, he was heading back to Washington, D.C. Truman was eating lunch when he received word of the Hiroshima bombing. The president then stood up and shook the hand of a captain who was serving as his luncheon companion. "Captain," Truman said, "this is the greatest thing in history."[14]

About 16 hours after Little Boy exploded above Japan, the American people learned about the bombing. Truman released a statement explaining that a new atomic weapon had been dropped on Hiroshima. He promised more destruction if the Japanese did not surrender: "If they do not now accept our terms they may expect a rain of ruin from the air, the like of which has never been seen on this earth."[15] The president also declared that the United States had "won the battle of the laboratories" just as it had won "the battles of the air, land, and sea."[16]

Like other people in the United States, the scientists at Los Alamos learned about the successful atomic bombing from the president's statement. Otto Frisch was working in a laboratory there when the news broke. He heard his fellow scientists running through the halls and yelling with excitement about how Little Boy had destroyed Hiroshima. Many of Frisch's friends rushed to call La Fonda Hotel in Santa Fe, eager to make reservations at its fancy restaurant so they could celebrate in style. After months or even years of hard work and endless worry, they were thrilled that the bomb had actually worked. Incredibly, their research and theories and sometimes-desperate guesses had all paid off. They had been assigned the nearly impossible goal of making an atomic bomb before the war's end, and they had done it.

Frisch understood their delight. Yet, as he later recalled, he still had a "feeling of unease, indeed nausea." As he explained, "[I]t seemed rather ghoulish to celebrate the sudden death of a hundred thousand people, even if they were 'enemies.'"[17] Frisch's remembrance of that moment suggested the complex emotions felt by many Manhattan Project participants once the exaltation wore off and reality set in.

Welcoming the Atomic Age

When it became clear that the Japanese would not surrender after the bombing of Hiroshima, the U.S. military prepared to make good on Truman's threat to destroy Japan. On August 7, some 6 million leaflets were dropped on 47 Japanese cities. They warned residents that the terrible weapon the United States had used on Hiroshima might soon be dropped on them. At the same time, the American troops on Tinian were hurriedly assembling Fat Man in preparation for the detonation of the first plutonium bomb in combat.

On August 9, Fat Man was placed in the bomb bay of *Bock's Car*, a B-29 piloted by Charles Sweeney. Sweeney's target was supposed to be a weapons arsenal in Kokura. Taking off in the early morning, *Bock's Car* circled above the city three times, but a thick cloud cover made it impossible for Sweeney to see his target. With his plane running low on fuel, he

Mamoru Shigemitsu, the Japanese Minister of Foreign Affairs at the end of World War II, signs the instrument of surrender for Emperor Hirohito of Japan aboard the USS *Missouri* on September 2, 1945.

decided to switch course and fly toward the back-up target of Nagasaki. Just as *Bock's Car* reached the city, the clouds broke and the crew dropped the bomb. Fat Man, exploding 1,700 feet (518 m) over the city, destroyed Nagasaki. About 40,000 of its residents were killed instantly. Eventually, the total death toll rose to 140,000.

Truman halted the shipping of a third atomic weapon as he waited to hear from the Japanese. After days of negotiation, Japan and the Allies agreed to terms of surrender on August 14, 1945. The next day, Emperor Hirohito of Japan addressed his people for the first time in a radio broadcast. "[T]he war situation has developed not necessarily to Japan's advantage," the emperor said, in a now famous understatement. "Moreover," he said, "the enemy has begun to employ a new and most cruel bomb, the power of which to do damage is indeed incalculable, taking the toll of many innocent lives."[1] World War II had finally come to an end. The atomic age, however, was only beginning.

LEARNING ABOUT THE BOMB

After years of incredibly tight security on its atomic bomb program, the U.S. government felt compelled to tell the public at least part of the story of the Manhattan Project. On August 12, it released *Atomic Energy for Military Purposes: The Official Report on the Development of the Atomic Bomb Under the Auspices of the United States Government, 1940–1945*. The document was popularly known as the Smyth Report, named after its author, Princeton physicist Henry DeWolf Smyth.

Groves had commissioned Smyth to write this history and description of the Manhattan Project. It was intended to satisfy public curiosity about the atomic bomb. At the same time, the report established for nuclear physicists what aspects of their work they could openly discuss. Scientists could assume that technical information not provided in the report was still considered top secret by the government.

The Smyth Report surprised many Americans, who could not believe that the U.S. government was able to operate a $2 billion program involving many thousands of people in absolute secret. Most stunned of all were the nontechnical employees at Oak Ridge, Hanford, and Los Alamos, who had had no idea that their wartime work was contributing to the creation of the atomic bomb.

MORAL QUESTIONS

Initially, most Americans approved of the bombing of Hiroshima and Nagasaki. They accepted the government's stance that the bomb's use against Japan was necessary to bring an end a horrific world war, which had killed tens of millions of

Servicemen in Times Square, New York, were thrilled to read newspaper extras announcing that Japan was ready to accept unconditional surrender if Emperor Hirohito would not be deposed. While Americans were elated that the war was finally over, many were later conflicted about the atomic bombing of Japan.

people worldwide. Some people, however, were not so comfortable with the bomb, including some prominent members of the U.S. military. For instance, General Dwight D. Eisenhower, who had served as the supreme commander of the Allied forces in Europe, believed that the Japanese would have surely surrendered even if Hiroshima and Nagasaki had not been destroyed. As he later said, "[I]t wasn't necessary to hit them with that awful thing."[2] Truman's chief of staff, Admiral

William D. Leahy, was also appalled by American conduct in the final days of the war. He said that the "use of this barbarous weapon at Hiroshima and Nagasaki was of no material assistance in our war against Japan. The Japanese were already defeated and ready to surrender. . . . [I]n being the first to use it, we . . . adopted an ethical standard common to the barbarians of the Dark Ages."[3]

Many of the scientists of the Manhattan Project were uneasy about the atomic age they had helped usher in. Oppenheimer, the man most instrumental in making the project a success, was also perhaps the most ambivalent about what they had done. In October 1945, Groves came to Los Alamos to award the laboratory a certificate of appreciation from the secretary of war. Oppenheimer marked the occasion with a speech that, in recounting his mixed feelings about the Manhattan Project, expressed the sentiments of many of his colleagues:

> It is our hope that in years to come we may look at this scroll, and all that it signifies, with pride.
>
> Today that pride must be tempered with a profound concern. If atomic bombs are to be added as new weapons to the arsenals of a warring world, or to the arsenals of nations preparing for war, then the time will come when mankind will curse the names of Los Alamos and Hiroshima.[4]

THE ACHESON-LILIENTHAL REPORT

In Washington, D.C., policymakers were concerned about the spread of nuclear warfare. For the moment, only the United States possessed the knowledge and resources to create atomic bombs. It was clear, however, that other nations, especially the USSR, would do everything in their power to build their own arsenals of these powerful weapons. Although Truman believed the Soviets were years away from obtaining their own atomic bombs, he wanted to know whether there was a way to avoid an expensive and dangerous international arms race.

Toward this end, he asked the Department of State to come up with a plan.

Undersecretary of State Dean Acheson was placed in charge of a committee to define American policy on atomic energy and weapons. The committee included Leslie R. Groves, Vannevar Bush, James Conant, and John McCloy. Acheson assembled a board of technical advisers, headed by David Lilienthal. Oppenheimer also served as a scientific consultant.

In March 1946, the committee released *The Report on the International Control of Atomic Energy*, better known as the Acheson-Lilienthal Report. Oppenheimer wrote much of the report, which called for the establishment of an international organization to oversee the production of fissionable material and the operation of all nuclear facilities around the world. Acknowledging the important peacetime uses of atomic research, it recommended that nations share information about nuclear energy. The report also stated that the United States would need to get rid of its existing atomic weapons, but it did not set a deadline for their destruction.

THE BARUCH PLAN

Truman called on presidential adviser Bernard Baruch to present these proposals to the United Nations, the international organization founded at the end of World War II to foster peaceful relations between countries. On June 14, 1946, Baruch spoke before the United Nations Atomic Energy Commission (UNAEC). At the beginning of his speech, he bluntly laid out what was stake:

> We are here to make a choice between the quick and the dead.
>> That is our business.
>> Behind the black portent of the new atomic age lies a hope which, seized upon with faith, can work our salvation. If we fail, then we have damned every man to be the slave of

Fear. Let us not deceive ourselves: We must elect World Peace or World Destruction.[5]

As he continued, Baruch delivered a modified version of the Acheson-Lilienthal Report, which became known as the Baruch Plan. It proposed the formation of the Atomic Development Authority to implement its proposals. Once the plan was set in motion, the United States promised to destroy its atomic weapons.

The USSR balked at the Baruch Plan. It did not want to give international inspectors the right to examine its nuclear facilities. It also resisted the idea of allowing the United States to retain its weapons for any length of time. The Baruch Plan came to a vote on December 30. Ten of the 12 countries represented on the UNAEC voted for it. The other two, the USSR and Poland, abstained. Because the vote was not unanimous, the measure was defeated.

The rejection of the Baruch Plan was a milestone in atomic policy. It ended the hope that the United States, the USSR, and other powers would be able to work to together to find a means of regulating nuclear technology. With no controls in place, an arms race was now inevitable.

DISMANTLING THE MANHATTAN PROJECT

While the government was forming atomic policy, it was also determining the fate of the Manhattan Project. Now that the war had ended, it was unclear what would become of Los Alamos. Many of the scientists there, however, did not want to wait and see. They instead were happy to return to civilian university posts now that their military mission—like the war itself—was over. Hans Bethe took a job at Cornell University, Enrico Fermi and Edward Teller went to the University of Chicago, George Kistiakowsky headed to Harvard University, and Glenn Seaborg and Emilio Segré found work at the University of California, Berkeley. Oppenheimer resigned from his post as director at Los Alamos, leaving U.S. Navy physicist Norris Bradbury to take his place. As Bethe explained:

> We all felt that, like the soldiers, we had done our duty and that we deserved to return to the type of work that we had chosen as our life's career, the pursuit of pure science and

ATOMS FOR PEACE

On December 8, 1953, President Dwight D. Eisenhower delivered to the General Assembly of the United Nations his "Atoms for Peace" speech. In one of the most important speeches of the Cold War era, Eisenhower tried to rally the nations of the world to work together to use nuclear research toward peaceful ends, such as producing nuclear energy, rather than to create ever more deadly weapons. As a result of "Atoms for Peace," the United Nations established the International Atomic Energy Agency (IAEA) in 1957 to monitor worldwide nuclear activities. Despite his appeal, Eisenhower was unable to slow the expanding arms race between the United States and the USSR:

> I would be prepared to submit to the Congress of the United States, and with every expectation of approval, any such plan that would, first, encourage world-wide investigation into the most effective peacetime uses of fissionable material, and with the certainty that the investigators had all the material needed for the conducting of all experiments that were appropriate; second, begin to diminish the potential destructive power of the world's atomic stockpiles; third, allow all peoples of all

teaching. . . . Moreover, it was not obvious in [1945 and] 1946 that there was any need for a large effort on atomic weapons in peacetime.[6]

Nuclear research at first did founder in the postwar era. By July 1946, however, Manhattan Project scientists were ready to test two slightly improved plutonium bombs built on the

nations to see that, in this enlightened age, the great Powers of the earth, both of the East and of the West, are interested in human aspirations first rather than in building up the armaments of war; fourth, open up a new channel for peaceful discussion and initiative at least a new approach to the many difficult problems that must be solved in both private and public conversations if the world is to shake off the inertia imposed by fear and is to make positive progress towards peace.

Against the dark background of the atomic bomb, the United States does not wish merely to present strength, but also the desire and the hope for peace. The coming months will be fraught with fateful decisions. In this Assembly, in the capitals and military headquarters of the world, in the hearts of men everywhere, be they governed or governors, may they be the decisions which will lead this world out of fear and into peace.

To the making of these fateful decisions, the United States pledges before you, and therefore before the world, its determination to help solve the fearful atomic dilemma— to devote its entire heart and mind to finding the way by which the miraculous inventiveness of man shall not be dedicated to his death, but consecrated to his life.*

* Dwight D. Eisenhower, "Atoms for Peace Speech." International Atomic Energy Agency. http://www.iaea.org/About/history_speech.html.

Fat Man model. As part of Operation Crossroads, the bombs were detonated at Bikini Atoll in the Marshall Islands in the Pacific Ocean. The U.S. Navy used the lagoon there to house old warships. During the Bikini tests, a large audience of military officers, congressmen, and journalists watched as the bombs were used to explode a collection of German, Japanese, and American vessels. (News accounts of the event inspired a French fashion designer to name his "explosive" two-piece bathing suit "the bikini.")

The Bikini tests were the last nuclear explosions under the auspices of the Manhattan Project. Over the objections of Leslie R. Groves, Congress removed military control over the nation's peacetime nuclear weapons program. After many months of debate, it passed the Atomic Energy Act, which was signed into law by Truman on August 1, 1946. The Atomic Energy Act established the United States Atomic Energy Commission (AEC). This commission, first headed by David Lilienthal, would oversee all nuclear research and atomic weapons development. Beginning on January 1, 1947, the duties of the Manhattan Engineer District were transferred to the AEC. Los Alamos remained a national laboratory, but, on August 15, 1947, the Manhattan Project—having achieved its wartime goals—officially came to an end.

The Legacy of the Manhattan Project

The Manhattan Project was formally disbanded 16 months after the war. Its influence, however, continued to be felt. In fact, it is not an exaggeration to say that human history can be divided into two periods—the time before the Manhattan Project and the time after. By introducing the atomic bomb, the Manhattan Project helped redefine the world as we know it. The project not only had a powerful impact on politics, war, environmental policy, scientific research, and popular culture, it also forever changed the way people thought about their lives and the world. Because of the Manhattan Project, people had to get used to an almost incomprehensible idea— that the planet and all life on it could be annihilated in a matter of seconds.

Dr. Hans Bethe of Cornell University, who was a member of the Manhattan Project, sits with other top U.S. physicists at Columbia University in New York on February 4, 1950. From left to right, front row: George B. Pegram, Samuel K. Allison, Bruno Rossi, and Dr. Bethe. Second row: Kenneth T. Bainbridge, Charles C. Lauritsen, Victor F. Weisskopf, and F. Wheeler Loomis. Last row, left to right: Robert B. Brode, Milton G. White, and Frederick Seitz. These scientists warned against the development of a hydrogen bomb, which would be far more deadly than the atomic bombs dropped on Japan.

THE ARMS RACE BEGINS

On September 23, 1949, the USSR made an announcement that chilled policymakers in Washington, D.C. The Soviets had created their own atomic bomb and successfully conducted a test explosion. The bomb, which Americans called Joe I after Soviet leader Joseph Stalin, was similar to the one detonated in July 1945 during the Trinity test. In a little more than four years, the nuclear program of the USSR had caught up with that of the United States.

Just as some Los Alamos scientists had warned, the United States and the USSR—then the two most powerful nations on Earth—entered a dangerous arms race to create ever more destructive nuclear weapons. Within months, President Truman was funneling resources into producing a thermonuclear bomb, also called a hydrogen bomb or H-bomb. Some research had been performed on the thermonuclear bomb during the Manhattan Project, but it was only a sideline. Now thermonuclear research was accelerated because it promised to produce more powerful bombs. The energy released in a thermonuclear bomb was created not by splitting atoms of uranium or plutonium (fission), but by combining atoms of hydrogen (fusion).

The United States detonated the world's first thermonuclear bomb in a test on November 1, 1952. The explosion was about 500 times larger than those produced by the atomic bombs dropped on Hiroshima and Nagasaki. The following year the USSR tested its first thermonuclear device. Throughout the next few decades, both nations worked to improve their nuclear bomb technology by creating better and smaller bomb designs. At the same time, they built more and more nuclear bombs, with each eventually amassing stockpiles of tens of thousands of weapons.

THE COLD WAR

This rivalry between the world's biggest nuclear powers created a period of strained relations now known as the Cold War (1945–1991). Unlike in a conventional war, the United States and the USSR did not actually attack each other during the Cold War era. The distrust and hostility between the two countries, however, suggested that a devastating conflict—one involving nuclear weapons—could break out at any time.

Cold War tensions reached their height during the Cuban Missile Crisis. On October 14, 1962, U.S. spy planes detected

Soviet missiles able to launch nuclear weapons on the island of Cuba, about 90 miles (145 km) from Florida. Major American cities, including New York, Chicago, and Los Angeles, were within the missiles' range.

President John F. Kennedy appeared on television and demanded that Premier Nikita Khrushchev remove the missiles. For several days, the world held its breath as the two nations remained in a tense standoff. Finally, on October 28, Khrushchev agreed to remove the Soviet weapons. The crisis was resolved, but few people, especially in the United States, could forget how close the world had come to seeing an all-out nuclear war.

A CULTURE OF FEAR

Part of the Manhattan Project's Cold War legacy was the culture of fear it inspired. Initially, Americans had overwhelmingly supported the atomic bombing of Japan, which many in the government believed was necessary to bring World War II to an end. Even so, many Americans grew uncomfortable as they learned more about the utter destructiveness of the bombs and the long-term suffering of the Japanese survivors of Hiroshima and Nagasaki.

A grim fascination with the bombings was evident in the reception of John Hersey's reportage from Hiroshima. In August 1946, the journalist's lengthy report about the personal experiences of six survivors appeared in the *New Yorker*; the issue sold out within hours. Later published as a book, *Hiroshima* became a best seller and won the Pulitzer Prize.

Fear of nuclear war soon became a staple theme of popular novels and films. *On the Beach* (1957), a book later made into a movie, told the story of Australian survivors of World War III waiting to die from radiation poisoning. The sober novel and film *Fail-Safe* (1964) imagined the consequences of an accidental nuclear attack on the USSR by the United States. The movie *Dr. Strangelove, or How I Learned to Stop*

Worrying and Love the Bomb (1964) recounted a similar tale but through the guise of black comedy. The Japanese film *Godzilla* (1954) and its sequels indirectly dealt with fears of nuclear radiation, which in the movies created a giant, city-destroying monster.

LOOKING FOR TRAITORS

The Manhattan Project also helped create a culture of paranoia in the United States. After the war, several scientists at Los Alamos, including Klaus Fuchs, were found guilty of passing nuclear weapons secrets to the USSR. In the most high-profile case, David Greenglass, a machinist at Los Alamos, was accused of giving his brother-in-law Julius Rosenberg crude drawings of atomic bombs, which Rosenberg then passed along to a Soviet courier. Rosenberg and his wife, Ethel, were found guilty of espionage in a highly publicized and controversial trial. Both were executed in the electric chair in 1953.

Fears grew that American Communists sympathetic to the USSR were infiltrating the government and influential industries. Exploiting these fears, Senator Joseph McCarthy rose to power in the 1950s by holding a series of hearings to root out supposed Communist sympathizers. In the end, the hearings ruined the lives of many innocent people who were falsely accused of being disloyal to their country.

One of the victims of the anti-Communist furor was J. Robert Oppenheimer, the former scientific director of Los Alamos. Many years before, Oppenheimer had been involved with the Communist Party, something Lieutenant General Leslie Groves had been fully aware of when he asked Oppenheimer to work on the Manhattan Project. By the early 1950s, however, some military figures were angered by Oppenheimer's very vocal opposition to the development of the hydrogen bomb. Citing his past association with Communists, they questioned his loyalty to the United States and had him stripped of his security clearance. Ironically, the man arguably most responsible for

On October 7, 1963, President John F. Kennedy signs the Limited Test Ban Treaty in the White House Treaty Room in Washington, D.C. Kennedy said the United States regarded the pact as a "clear and honorable national commitment to the cause of man's survival." The treaty, signed by Britain and the Soviet Union, prohibits nuclear weapon test explosions in the atmosphere, in outer space, and underwater, but not underground.

creating the American nuclear program was barred from working on it.

CHANGING SCIENTIFIC RESEARCH

Another significant legacy of the Manhattan Project is how it changed science and scientific research. In the early twentieth century, most research was conducted at universities or by specialized scientific organizations. Individuals or small teams of scientists working in modest laboratories often made groundbreaking discoveries. For instance, Ernest Rutherford was able to perform his pioneering research into the structure of the atom largely working alone and using equipment that required no more space than a tabletop. In contrast, state-of-the-art physics research now generally requires enormous machines and hundreds of scientists working with multinational organizations.

The Manhattan Project was a turning point in the transition from what became known as "Little Science" to "Big Science." The $2-billion Manhattan Project provided a model of how the government, coupled with industry, could quickly advance scientific research by steering money and resources toward a central goal. Just as important, it changed the relationship between science and government. Suddenly, in the postwar era, scientists and their work were seen as crucial to national security, not only in the United States, but in the USSR and other powerful countries as well. As a result, in the late twentieth century, many nations began to pour state funds, often funneled through the military, into scientific research that might generate new types of weapons or defense systems.

The Manhattan Project also introduced a new term into the English language. Now, "Manhattan Project" is routinely applied to government programs that have nothing to do with the atomic bomb. The term has become a shorthand way of describing any governmental effort to solve a serious problem by devoting vast amounts of money, attention, and manpower to it. For instance, in recent years, policymakers and activists have called for "Manhattan Projects" to address climate change, develop alternative energy sources, reform the health care industry, and improve the economy. Although the actual Manhattan Project was carried out in complete secrecy, demands for new "Manhattan Projects" are usually presented as public calls-to-arms, requiring the participation of all citizens in a grand project as a test of the national character.

NUCLEAR TECHNOLOGY IN PEACETIME

By forwarding nuclear research and discovering ways of isolating radioactive materials, the Manhattan Project was instrumental in furthering several new fields of science. One of the most promising is nuclear medicine. This specialty uses radioactive substances to help diagnose and treat illnesses and injuries. For instance, a patient may be injected with a substance that emits trace amounts of radioactivity. A scanner can use this emission to create a visual image of internal organs. MRI (magnetic resonance imaging) machines employ nuclear technology to create full body scans. Such diagnostic tests help doctors detect problems and disorders long before physical symptoms appear, allowing patients to begin treatment before significant damage has occurred. Radioactive substances are also commonly used to kill diseased cells in the treatment of certain cancers.

An even more far-reaching consequence of atomic bomb technology is the advent of nuclear power as a major source of energy. Working on the Manhattan Project at the Met Lab at the University of Chicago, Enrico Fermi created a primitive nuclear reactor in 1942. He used it to produce the first controlled nuclear chain reaction, thereby proving that humankind could harness the energy of the atom for its own use. Two years later, the first large-scale nuclear reactors were built at the Manhattan Project's plutonium plant at Hanford, Washington.

After the war, President Eisenhower promoted the development of nuclear energy around the world in his now-famous "Atoms for Peace" speech. The military community in the

United States, however, resisted sharing reactor research for fear that it would spread technology that other countries could adapt to create nuclear bombs. Nevertheless, in the 1950s, nuclear power plants began operating in the United States, the USSR, and Europe. The U.S. Navy also pioneered the use of nuclear energy to power submarines and aircraft carriers. The USS *Nautilus*, the navy's first nuclear-powered sub, made its maiden voyage in 1954.

THE DOWNSIDE OF NUCLEAR ENERGY

Initially, nuclear energy seemed almost too good to be true. It offered a clean alternative to fossil fuels, such as coal and oil, which produce air pollution when burned. It also promised to be a cheap source of power that could lower the cost of electricity worldwide. These high hopes faded, however, as people became more worried about the safety of nuclear power plants. In the United States, these concerns spawned a widespread anti-nuclear power movement, especially after 1979, when an accident at the nuclear reactor on Three Mile Island near Harrisburg, Pennsylvania, released a small amount of radioactive gas. The event turned many Americans against nuclear energy, as they came to believe that the risks it posed far outweighed its benefits.

In 1986, a much more serious accident in the USSR drew international attention to safety issues surrounding nuclear power. A reactor in the town of Chernobyl exploded, sending radioactive substances through the air as far away as northern Europe. The worst nuclear power plant accident in history, the incident forced a large evacuation and massive cleanup of the contaminated environment. Many cancer deaths and other health problems have been linked to Chernobyl.

Many people opposed nuclear energy, not only because of possible reactor accidents, but also because of the waste it produces. Nuclear waste stays radioactive for thousands of

(continues on page 108)

JOSEPH ROTBLAT (1908–2005)

Winner of the 1995 Nobel Peace Prize, Joseph Rotblat was the only scientist to quit the Manhattan Project because of a moral objection to the creation of the atomic bomb. Born on November 4, 1908, in Warsaw, Poland, Rotblat went to work as an electrician at 15. He dreamed of becoming a physicist and spent his nights studying to achieve that goal. After receiving a doctorate from University of Warsaw, he was invited by the distinguished British physicist James Chadwick to work at his laboratory in Liverpool, England. Because of his low pay, Rotblat was unable to take his wife, Tola, with him. After the German army invaded Poland in September 1939 and ignited World War II, Rotblat never heard from her again. He remained single for the rest of his life.

Rotblat was one of a group 19 physicists in England sent to Los Alamos, New Mexico, to work on the Manhattan Project. Rotblat was willing to help the American military build an atomic bomb because he believed the threat of using the weapon against Germany would prevent the Germans from designing and using their own atomic bomb. Soon after arriving in Los Alamos, however, Rotblat learned that, according to American intelligence agents, German scientists were nowhere near creating the bomb. Without the German threat, Rotblat turned against the Manhattan Project. He maintained that it would be immoral for the United States to continue to develop the atomic bomb for use against Japan. He also objected to the idea of bombing Japan to intimidate the USSR. After nine months with the Manhattan Project, Rotblat quit his job and returned to

England. American intelligence agents accused him of being a Soviet spy. Even after he convinced them he was not, he was not allowed to return to the United States for years.

In 1949, Rotblat became a professor of physics at the medical college of St. Bartholomew's Hospital in London. He remained in that post until his retirement in 1976. Rotblat's research there focused on the medical effects of exposure to radiation. In 1955, Rotblat became one of 11 eminent scientists and intellectuals to sign the Russell-Einstein Manifesto. The document—named after its authors, philosopher Bertrand Russell and physicist Albert Einstein—warned of the dangers of nuclear warfare and called on all nations to resolve conflicts peacefully. It also proposed an international conference at which scientists and public figures could openly discuss issues involving nuclear weapons without regard to politics.

Rotblat was instrumental in organizing such a conference two years later in Pugwash, Nova Scotia, in Canada. It was just the first of hundreds of meetings that became known as the Pugwash Conferences on Sciences and World Affairs. Serving as secretary-general and later president of the Pugwash Conferences, Rotblat worked toward the group's ultimate goal—the elimination of nuclear weapons. At the same time, Rotblat promoted international treaties to reduce the spread of these weapons and to ban atomic weapons testing. For his efforts, Rotblat was awarded the Nobel Peace Prize, which he shared with the Pugwash organization, in 1995, the year that marked the fiftieth anniversary of the bombings of Hiroshima and Nagasaki. Rotblat continued to lecture on the dangers of nuclear weapons until his death on August 31, 2005.

(continued from page 105)

years. For health safety, it needs to be properly stored underground. There have been a number of accidents in which waste has escaped and contaminated rivers, lakes, and other water sources. Environmentalists are also concerned about radiation leaks occurring when waste is transported to a storage site.

FIGHTING THE SPREAD OF NUCLEAR WEAPONS

In the late twentieth century, while concerns about the safety of nuclear energy grew, so did fears about the spread of nuclear weapons technology. In 1968, international diplomats negotiated the Treaty on the Non-Proliferation of Nuclear Weapons. The treaty divided the world into nuclear states (countries that had nuclear weapons) and non-nuclear states (those that did not). At the time, there were five nuclear states: the United States, Great Britain, the USSR, France, and China. By the terms of the treaty, they promised not to assist any non-nuclear states in obtaining nuclear weapons. The non-nuclear states that signed the treaty pledged not to attempt to acquire nuclear weapons or to manufacture them. They also agreed to comply with inspections of their nuclear activities by the International Atomic Energy Agency (IAEA), which was established in 1957.

Many hoped that the treaty would reduce the threat of nuclear war, a hope that was further stoked by the collapse of the USSR in 1991, which marked the end of the Cold War. Despite these developments, however, nuclear weapons continued to pose significant dangers to world peace. By the late 1990s, India and Pakistan, neither of which had signed the nonproliferation treaty, had become nuclear states. The two countries were involved in an ongoing territorial dispute over the Kashmir region, which raised fears that these tensions could erupt into a regional nuclear war.

According to some scientists, even a limited nuclear conflict would cause a worldwide catastrophe. In the mid-1980s, they introduced the concept of nuclear winter. According to their controversial theory, a nuclear exchange could have a dire effect on climate across the globe. If a series of nuclear explosions produced enough smoke and dust, it could block out sunlight long enough to dramatically drop global temperatures and destroy all plant life.

Growing fears of nuclear proliferation helped fuel the U.S. military's invasion of Iraq in 2003. The U.S. government justified the war by insisting Iraq was trying to obtain nuclear weapons, although evidence of that claim was never found. Some international experts worried that this "pre-emptive" war would inspire non-nuclear states to seek out nuclear weapons for self-protection.

Concerns escalated when North Korea, led by the erratic dictator Kim Jong Il, withdrew from the nonproliferation treaty in 2003. Three years later, North Korea tested its first nuclear weapon. The event brought the number of known nuclear states up to eight, although Israel is also thought to possess nuclear weapons. The number of nuclear states remains smaller than many past experts had feared. Nevertheless, the IAEA estimates that as many as 30 other nations already have the technological capability to initiate a nuclear bomb program if they choose to do so.

Nonproliferation efforts are also challenged by some non-state organizations, especially terrorist groups. Since the terrorist attacks of September 11, 2001, fears have risen that a terrorist organization could purchase a nuclear weapon on the black market. With the spread of nuclear technology, it is also possible that, if a terrorist group could acquire enough uranium or plutonium, it might amass the expertise to build a nuclear weapon on its own.

ASSESSING THE MANHATTAN PROJECT

In 1994, the Smithsonian National Air and Space Museum in Washington, D.C., was preparing to launch a new exhibit. Timed for display on the fiftieth anniversary of the bombing of Hiroshima and Nagasaki, it was titled "The Crossroads: The End of World War II, the Atomic Bomb and the Cold War." Before its installation, however, a draft of the exhibition's text caused a firestorm. Groups of World War II veterans, some members of Congress, and even Paul W. Tibbets, the pilot of the plane that dropped the bomb on Hiroshima, denounced the exhibit. They said it diminished the heroism of American soldiers during the war and overemphasized the horrific destruction caused by the atomic bombs.

The critics were livid that the exhibit presented the views of some historians who maintained that President Truman was wrong to order the bombing. For decades after the war, the historical consensus held that the bombings had prevented the invasion of Japan and saved many thousands, if not millions, of lives. Many later scholars, however, argued that the Japanese were close to surrender and would have surrendered without the destruction of Hiroshima and Nagasaki.

The brouhaha over the exhibit grew so intense that the museum issued its own surrender. In the end, the exhibit's text was reworked so as not to offend anyone on either side. The exhibit may have been watered down, but the controversy still remains heated among scholars and students of the war. Was the atomic bombing of Japan a necessary measure to end a vicious war, or was it a black mark on American history that ushered in the dark and dangerous atomic age?

The program that produced the first atomic weapons also inspires troubling questions. For instance, Richard Rhodes, a renowned scholar of the atomic bomb, asked in a 2007 article, "Should Americans be proud of the Manhattan Project's work? Should we be ashamed?"[1] Given the Manhattan Project's history and legacy, answering these simple questions is anything but easy. On one hand, we can see the Manhattan Project as an amazing scientific and technological achievement born out of good and noble intentions. At a time when much of Europe was dominated by Adolf Hitler, whose fascist beliefs led to the systematic murder of millions of people throughout Europe, the program brought together a group of international scientists who worked tirelessly to create the one thing they believed could stop a madman bent on world domination. On the other hand, we can also view the Manhattan Project as an enterprise that unleashed on the world a weapon so devastating it could kill all life in a matter of minutes. Despite decades of effort to control this threat, the nightmare of nuclear holocaust will likely haunt our thoughts for as long humanity exists.

CHRONOLOGY

1897   J.J. Thomson discovers the electron, the first known subatomic particle.

1919   Ernest Rutherford discovers the proton.

1932   James Chadwick discovers the neutron.

1939   **January 26** Niels Bohr announces the discovery of the fission process during a meeting on theoretical physics in Washington, D.C.

        August 2 Albert Einstein writes President Franklin D. Roosevelt to urge him to fund research on the atomic bomb.

TIMELINE

1939
August 2 Albert Einstein writes President Franklin D. Roosevelt to urge him to fund research on the atomic bomb.

1943
August 19 In the Quebec Agreement, the United States and Great Britain agree to collaborate on the development of the atomic bomb.

1939 ———————— **1943**

1941
July 15 British physicists state in the MAUD Report that the creation of an atomic bomb is feasible.

1942
January Roosevelt approves a government project to produce the atomic bomb.
August The Manhattan Engineer District (also known as the Manhattan Project) is established.

1939   September Germany invades Poland; World War II begins.

1941   February Glenn T. Seaborg identifies the radioactive element plutonium.

July 15 British physicists state in the MAUD Report that the creation of an atomic bomb is feasible.

December The Japanese attack Pearl Harbor; the United States enters World War II.

1942   January Roosevelt approves a government project to produce the atomic bomb.

August The Manhattan Engineer District (also known as the Manhattan Project) is established; Colonel James C. Marshall is placed in charge.

1945
February–March The designs of the Little Boy and Fat Man bombs are finalized.
May–June The Interim Committee recommends the U.S. military use of atomic weapons against Japan.
July Los Alamos scientists perform the Trinity test of the plutonium bomb at Alamogordo, New Mexico.

1945   1947

August 6 The United States drops Little Boy, a uranium bomb, on Hiroshima, Japan.
August 9 The United States drops Fat Man, a plutonium bomb, on Nagasaki, Japan.
August 14 Japan surrenders; World War II ends.

1947
August 15 The Manhattan Project comes to an end.

1942   **September** Leslie R. Groves takes over the management of the Manhattan Project; he selects Oak Ridge, Tennessee, as the site for plants to produce fissionable uranium.

November Groves selects Los Alamos, New Mexico, as the site of the Manhattan Project's central laboratory.

December 2 Fermi achieves the first man-made nuclear chain reaction at the Metallurgical Laboratory at the University of Chicago.

1943   **January** Groves selects Hanford, Washington, as the site for a plutonium-producing facility.

March Director J. Robert Oppenheimer welcomes Manhattan Project scientists to the Los Alamos laboratory.

August 19 In the Quebec Agreement, the United States and Great Britain agree to collaborate on the development of the atomic bomb.

September 3 Italy surrenders to the Allied forces.

1944   **July** Los Alamos researchers reject the Thin Man bomb design.

1945   **February-March** The designs of the Little Boy and Fat Man bombs are finalized.

May 7 Germany surrenders, ending World War II in Europe.

May-June The Interim Committee recommends the U.S. military use of atomic weapons against Japan.

June Scientists at the Met Lab issue the Franck Report; the Interim Committee rejects the Franck Report's plea not to bomb Japan.

July Los Alamos scientists perform the Trinity test of the plutonium bomb at Alamogordo, New Mexico.

1945   **July-August** Allied leaders President Harry S. Truman, Prime Minister Churchill, and Premier Joseph Stalin meet in Potsdam, Germany; Truman issues the Potsdam Proclamation.

August 6 The United States drops Little Boy, a uranium bomb, on Hiroshima, Japan.

August 9 The United States drops Fat Man, a plutonium bomb, on Nagasaki, Japan.

August 12 The Smyth Report reveals information about the Manhattan Project to the American public.

August 14 Japan surrenders; World War II ends.

1946   **June 14** The Baruch Plan is presented to the United Nations Atomic Energy Commission.

July Operation Crossroads demonstrates the plutonium bomb at Bikini Atoll.

August 1 Truman signs the Atomic Energy Act of 1946.

1947   **August 15** The Manhattan Project comes to an end.

NOTES

CHAPTER 1

1. Richard Rhodes, *The Making of the Atomic Bomb*. New York: Simon & Schuster, 1986, p. 657.
2. Cynthia C. Kelly, ed., *The Manhattan Project: The Birth of the Atomic Bomb in the Words of Its Creators, Eyewitnesses, and Historians*. New York: Black Dog & Leventhal Publishers, 2007, p. 298.
3. Rhodes, p. 666.
4. Ibid.
5. Kelly, p. 297.
6. Ibid., p. 294.
7. Rhodes, p. 668.
8. Ibid.
9. Ibid., p. 672.
10. Ibid., p. 673.
11. Kelly, p. 296.
12. Rhodes, p. 672.
13. Kelly, p. 295.
14. Rhodes, p. 676.
15. Ibid.
16. Ibid.

CHAPTER 2

1. Richard Rhodes, *The Making of the Atomic Bomb*. New York: Simon & Schuster, 1986, p. 66.
2. Ibid., p. 165.
3. Ibid.
4. Ibid., pp. 27–28.
5. Ibid., p. 28.
6. Ibid., p. 261.
7. Ibid., p. 267.

CHAPTER 3

1. Richard Rhodes, *The Making of the Atomic Bomb*. New York: Simon & Schuster, 1986, p. 280.
2. Ibid., p. 294.
3. Ibid., p. 315.
4. Ibid., p. 317.
5. Cynthia C. Kelly, ed., *The Manhattan Project: The Birth of the Atomic Bomb in the Words of Its Creators, Eyewitnesses, and Historians*. New York: Black Dog & Leventhal Publishers, 2007, p. 46.
6. Ibid.
7. Rhodes, p. 337.
8. Ibid., p. 361.
9. Ibid., p. 369.

CHAPTER 4

1. Cynthia C. Kelly, ed., *The Manhattan Project: The Birth of the Atomic Bomb in the Words of Its Creators, Eyewitnesses, and Historians*. New York: Black Dog & Leventhal Publishers, 2007, p. 121.
2. Ibid., p. 84.
3. Ibid., p. 91.
4. Richard Rhodes, *The Making of the Atomic Bomb*. New York: Simon & Schuster, 1986, p. 499.
5. Ibid., pp. 447–448.
6. Ibid., p. 448.
7. Ibid., p. 452.
8. Ibid.

CHAPTER 5

1. Los Alamos National Laboratory, "Life During the War." http://www.lanl.gov/history/wartime/duringwar.shtml.

2. Richard Rhodes, *The Making of the Atomic Bomb*. New York: Simon & Schuster, 1986, p. 565.

3. Ibid., p. 524.

CHAPTER 6

1. Richard Rhodes, *The Making of the Atomic Bomb*. New York: Simon & Schuster, 1986, p. 697.

2. Ibid., p. 749.

3. Ibid., p. 697.

4. Ibid.

5. F.G. Gosling, *The Manhattan Project: Making the Atomic Bomb*. Washington, D.C.: History Division, Department of Energy, 1999, p. 50.

6. Ibid.

7. Rhodes, p. 690.

8. Gosling, p. 51.

9. Cynthia C. Kelly, ed., *The Manhattan Project: The Birth of the Atomic Bomb in the Words of Its Creators, Eyewitnesses, and Historians*. New York: Black Dog & Leventhal Publishers, 2007, p. 317.

10. Rhodes, p. 700.

11. Kelly, p. 330.

12. Rhodes, p. 711.

13. Ibid., pp. 717–718.

14. Kelly, p. 331.

15. Ibid., p. 341.

16. Ibid., p. 340.

17. Rhodes, pp. 735–736.

CHAPTER 7

1. Richard Rhodes, *The Making of the Atomic Bomb*. New York: Simon & Schuster, 1986, p. 745.

2. Cynthia C. Kelly, ed., *The Manhattan Project: The Birth of the Atomic Bomb in the Words of Its Creators, Eyewitnesses, and Historians*. New York: Black Dog & Leventhal Publishers, 2007, p. 415.

3. Ibid.

4. Rhodes, p. 758.

5. "Bernard Baruch, Speech Before the United Nations Atomic Energy Commission (June 14, 1946)." http://www.honors.umd.edu/HONR269J/archive/Baruch Plan.html.

6. Rhodes, p. 754.

CHAPTER 8

1. Richard Rhodes, "Why We Should Preserve the Manhattan Project," *Bulletin of the Atomic Scientists* 63 (May/June 2007), p. 36.

BIBLIOGRAPHY

Fermi, Rachel. *Picturing the Bomb: Photographs from the Secret World of the Manhattan Project*. New York: Harry N. Abrams, 1995.

Gosling, F.G. *The Manhattan Project: Making the Atomic Bomb*. Washington, D.C.: History Division, Department of Energy, 1999.

Hales, Peter B. *Atomic Spaces: Living on the Manhattan Project*. Urbana: University of Illinois Press, 1997.

Hughes, Jeff. *The Manhattan Project: Big Science and the Atom Bomb*. New York: Columbia University Press, 2002.

Kelly, Cynthia C., ed. *The Manhattan Project: The Birth of the Atomic Bomb in the Words of Its Creators, Eyewitnesses, and Historians*. New York: Black Dog & Leventhal Publishers, 2007.

———. *Remembering the Manhattan Project: Perspectives on the Making of the Atomic Bomb and Its Legacy*. Hackensack, N.J.: World Scientific, 2004.

Rhodes, Richard. *The Making of the Atomic Bomb*. New York: Simon & Schuster, 1986.

FURTHER RESOURCES

BOOKS

Hersey, John. *Hiroshima*. 1946. Reprint, New York: Vintage Books, 1989.

Pasachoff, Naomi. *Niels Bohr: Physicist and Humanitarian*. Berkeley Heights, N.J.: Enslow Publishers, 2003.

Scherer, Glenn, and Marty Fletcher. *J. Robert Oppenheimer: The Brain Behind the Bomb*. Berkeley Heights, N.J.: MyReportLinks.com, 2007.

Sherrow, Victoria. *The Making of the Atom Bomb*. San Diego: Lucent Books, 2000.

Stux, Erica. *Enrico Fermi: Trailblazer in Nuclear Physics*. Berkeley Heights, N.J.: Enslow Publishers, 2004.

Sullivan, Edward T. *The Ultimate Weapon: The Race to Develop the Atomic Bomb*. New York: Holiday House, 2007.

Ziff, John. *The Bombing of Hiroshima*. Philadelphia: Chelsea House Publishers, 2001.

WEB SITES

The Atomic Heritage Foundation
http://www.atomicheritage.org

Hiroshima Peace Memorial Museum: A-Bomb Survivors Exhibit
http://www.pcf.city.hiroshima.jp/BPW/english/index.html

Los Alamos National Laboratory: History
http://www.lanl.gov/history/index.shtml

The Manhattan Project: An Interactive History
http://www.cfo.doe.gov/me70/manhattan/index.htm

The National Museum of Nuclear Science & History
http://www.nuclearmuseum.org/online-museum

New York Times, Voices of the Manhattan Project
http://www.nytimes.com/interactive/2008/10/28/science/
28manhattanproject.html?ref=science

Nuclear Age Peace Foundation: Manhattan Project
http://www.nuclearfiles.org/menu/key-issues/
nuclear-weapons/history/pre-cold-war/manhattan-project/
index.htm

Trinity Remembered
http://www.trinityremembered.com/index.html

PICTURE CREDITS

PAGE

9: Los Alamos National Lab/
 Getty Images
18: Alamy
22: The Granger Collection
26: SSPL/Getty Images
29: Science & Society Picture
 Library/SSPL/Getty Images
39: March Of Time/March Of
 Time/Time Life Pictures/
 Getty Images
49: Alamy
53: AP Images

56: AP Images
65: AP Images
68: AP Images
70: AP Images
76: U.S. Navy/AP Images
80: U.S. Air Force/AP Images
84: Roger Viollet/Getty Images
88: AP Images
90: Harry Harris/AP Images
98: Harry Harris/AP Images
102: AP Images

INDEX

ABOUT THE AUTHOR

LIZ SONNEBORN is a writer living in Brooklyn, New York. A graduate of Swarthmore College, she has written more than 80 books for children and adults. Her works include *The American West*, *The California Gold Rush*, *Yemen*, *A to Z of American Indian Women*, and *The Ancient Kushites*, which the African Studies Association's Children's Africana Book Awards named an Honor Book for Older Readers in 2006.